MW00636679

WAR, TERRIBLE WAR
1855–1865

TEACHING GUIDE
FOR THE REVISED 3RD EDITION

OXFORD
UNIVERSITY PRESS

OXFORD
UNIVERSITY PRESS

Oxford University Press, Inc., publishes works that
further Oxford University's objective of excellence
in research, scholarship, and education.

Oxford   New York
Auckland   Cape Town   Dar es Salaam   Hong Kong   Karachi
Kuala Lumpur   Madrid   Melbourne   Mexico City   Nairobi
New Delhi   Shanghai   Taipei   Toronto

With offices in
Argentina   Austria   Brazil   Chile   Czech Republic   France   Greece
Guatemala   Hungary   Italy   Japan   Poland   Portugal   Singapore
South Korea   Switzerland   Thailand   Turkey   Ukraine   Vietnam

Copyright © 2003 by Oxford University Press

Writers: Joan Poole, Deborah Parks, Karen Edwards
Editors: Robert Weisser, Susan Moger
Editorial Consultant: Susan Buckley

Revision Copyright © 2005 by Oxford University Press, Inc.

Published by Oxford University Press, Inc.
198 Madison Avenue, New York, New York, 10016
www.oup.com

Oxford is a registered trademark of Oxford University Press

All rights reserved. No part of this publication may be reproduced,
stored in a retrieval system, or transmitted in any form or by any means,
electronic, mechanical, photocopying, recording, or otherwise,
without the prior permission of Oxford University Press.

ISBN-13: 978-0-19-522310-1 (California edition)   ISBN-13: 978-0-19-518891-2

Project Editor: Matt Fisher
Project Director: Jacqueline A. Ball
Education Consultant: Diane L. Brooks, Ed.D.

Casper Grathwohl, Publisher

Printed in the United States
on acid-free paper

CONTENTS

Note from the Author   4

HOW TO USE THIS TEACHING GUIDE

The *History of US* Program   6

Improving Literacy with *A History of US*   14–19

Reading History   14

Using the Johns Hopkins Team Learning Activities   15

TEACHING STRATEGIES FOR BOOK SIX

Historical Overview   21

Introducing the Book with Projects and Activities   24

Part 1: A Terrible Remedy (Preface I–Chapter 2)   27

Part 2: A Growing Crisis (Chapters 3–10)   36

Part 3: The South Secedes (Chapters 11–14)   50

Part 4: A House Divided (Chapters 15–17)   59

Part 5: Ordeal by Fire (Chapters 18–26)   67

Part 6: An End—And a Beginning
  (Chapters 27–31)   81

Synthesizing the Big Ideas in Book Six   91

APPENDIX

Part Check-Ups   93

Resource Pages   99

Maps

Rubrics

Graphic Organizers

Answer Key   130

NOTE FROM THE AUTHOR

Dear Teacher,

It is through story that people have traditionally passed on their ideas, their values, and their heritage. In recent years, however, we have come to think of stories as the property of the youngest of our children. How foolish of us. The rejection of story has made history seem dull. It has turned it into a litany of facts and dates. Stories make the past understandable (as well as enjoyable). Stories tell us who we are and where we've been. Without knowledge of our past, we can't make sense of the present.

As a former teacher, I knew of the need for a narrative history for young people, so I sat down and wrote one. (It took me seven years.) I was tired of seeing children struggle with arm-breaking, expensive books. I wanted my books to be inexpensive, light in weight, and user-friendly. Thanks to creative partnering by American Historical Publications and Oxford University Press, that's the way they are.

Called *A History of US,* mine is a set of 11 books. My hope is that they will help make American history—our story—a favorite subject again. It is important that it be so. As we prepare for the 21st century, we are becoming an increasingly diverse people. While we need to celebrate and enjoy that diversity, we also need to find solid ground to stand on together. Our history can provide that commonality. We are a nation built on ideas, on great documents, on individual achievement—and none of that is the property of any one group of us. Harriet Tubman, Abraham Lincoln, Emily Dickinson, Sequoya, and Duke Ellington belong to all of us—and so do our horse thieves, slave owners, and robber barons. We need to consider them all.

Now, to be specific, what do I intend these books to do in your classrooms? First of all, I want to help turn your students into avid readers. I want them to understand that nonfiction can be as exciting as fiction. (Besides, it is the kind of reading they'll meet most in the adult world.) I want to stretch their minds. I've written stories, but the stories are true stories. In nonfiction you grapple with the real world. I want to help children understand how fascinating that process can be.

I've tried to design books that I would have liked as a teacher—books that are flexible, easy-to-read, challenging, and idea-centered, that will lead children into energetic discussions. History can do that. It involves issues we still argue about. It gives us material with which to make judgments. It allows for comparisons. It hones the mind.

People all over this globe are dying—literally—because they want to live under a democracy. We've got the world's model and most of us don't understand or appreciate it. I want to help children learn about their country so they will be intelligent citizens. I want them to understand the heritage that they share with all the diverse people who are us—the citizens of the United States.

For some of your students, these books may be an introduction to history. What they actually remember will be up to you. Books can inspire and excite, but understanding big ideas and remembering details takes some reinforced learning. You'll find many suggestions for that in this Teaching Guide.

What you do with *A History of Us* and this Teaching Guide will depend, of course, on you and your class. You may have students read every chapter or only some chapters, many volumes or only a few. (But, naturally, I hope they'll read it all. Our history makes good reading.) I hope you'll use the books to teach reading and thinking skills as well as history and geography. We need to stop thinking of subjects as separate from each other. We talk about integrating the curriculum; we need to really do it. History, broadly, is the story of a culture—and that embraces art, music, science, mathematics, and literature. (You'll find some of all of those in these books.)

Reading *A History of Us* is easy; even young children seem to enjoy it. But some of the concepts in the books are not easy. They can be challenging to adults, which means that the volumes can be read on several levels. The idea is to get students excited by history and stretched mentally—at whatever their level of understanding. (Don't worry if every student doesn't understand every word. We adults don't expect that of our reading; we should allow for the same variety of comprehension among student readers.)

This Teaching Guide is filled with ideas meant to take the students back to the text to do a careful, searching read. It will also send them out to do research and writing and discovering on their own. The more you involve your students, the more they will understand and retain. Confucius, one of the worlds' great teachers, had this to say:

Tell me and I will forget. Show me and I will remember. Involve me and I will understand.

History is about discovering. It is a voyage that you and your students can embark on together. I wish you good sailing.

Joy Hakim with two of her favorite readers, her grandchildren, Natalie and Sam Johnson

Joy Hakim

THE HISTORY OF US PROGRAM

I. STUDENT EDITION

- By Joy Hakim, winner of James Michener Prize in Writing
- Engaging, friendly narrative
- A wide range of primary sources in every chapter
- Period illustrations and specially commissioned maps
- New atlas section customized for each book

II. TEACHING GUIDE

- Standards-based instruction
- Wide range of activities and classroom approaches
- Strategies for universal access and improving literacy (ELL, struggling readers, advanced learners)
- Multiple assessment tools

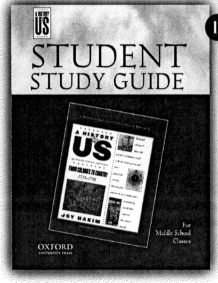

III. STUDENT STUDY GUIDE

- Exercises correlated to Student Edition and Teaching Guide
- Portfolio approach
- Activities for every level of learning
- Literacy through reading and writing
- Completely new for 2005

SOURCEBOOK AND INDEX

- Broad selection of primary sources in each subject area
- Ideal resource for in-class exercises and unit projects

Each Teaching Guide is organized into Parts. Each Part includes Chapter Lessons, a Team Learning Project from Johns Hopkins University, Check-up Tests, and other assessments and activities

PARTS
Unify chapter lessons with themes and projects.

INTRODUCTION
▶ Lists standards addressed in each chapter
▶ Gives objectives and big ideas and suggests projects and lessons to set context for the chapters

SUMMARY
▶ Gives assessment ideas and debate, ethics, and interdisciplinary project ideas

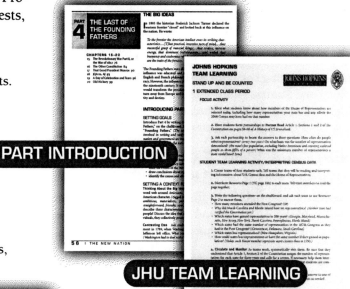

PART INTRODUCTION

JHU TEAM LEARNING

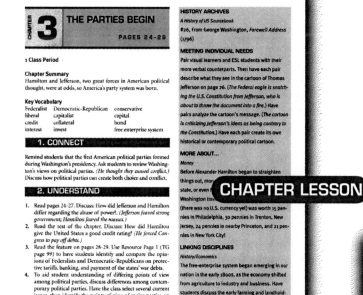

CHAPTER LESSON

JHU TEAM LEARNING
▶ Each Part contains a cooperative learning project developed by the Talent Development Middle School Program at Johns Hopkins University specifically for *A History of US*.

CHAPTER LESSONS
▶ Correlated to the new Student Study Guide
▶ Ideas for enrichment, discussion, writing, vocabulary, and projects

RUBRICS, CHECK-UPS, AND RESOURCE PAGES
▶ Reproduce and hand out for assessment and activities

CHECK-UP

RESOURCE PAGE

RUBRICS

SET A CONTEXT FOR READING

The books in *A History of US* are written so that a student can read them from cover to cover. You can strengthen students' connection to major themes through introductory lessons or projects. These lessons can be found in the introduction to the Teaching Guide and the opening pages for each Part.

Some students, especially developing readers or those learning English as a second language, may need extra help building background knowledge before reading the text. For these students, exercises in the Teaching and Student Study Guides help to set a context for reading. Look for **Connect** (in the Teaching Guide) and **Access** (in the Student Study Guide) sections. Also, refer to the Improving Literacy section (pages 20–25) for general strategies from an expert.

CREATE A FLEXIBLE CLASSROOM PLAN USING THE STUDENT STUDY GUIDE AND TEACHING GUIDE

The ancillary materials for *A History of US* have been developed for multiple teaching strategies, depending on the particular needs and abilities of your students. Choose an approach that works best for your students. Here are a few options:

▶ **Assign Student Study Guide activities as best suits your class needs**
The Student Study Guide activities are designed to reinforce and clarify content. They were created for students to complete with a minimum of explanation or supervision. The Student Study Guide can be used as homework or in class. The activities can be assigned concurrently with the reading, to help comprehend the material and come to class ready for in-depth discussion of the reading, or as a follow-up to the reading.

▶ **Use Teaching Guide activities to build and enrich comprehension**
The activities from the **Understand** section of each Chapter Lesson, as well as the sidebars, are meant to foster a dynamic, active, vocal classroom. They center on participatory small group and partner projects and focused individual work.

▶ **Use group projects to broaden understanding**
Other suggestions for group projects are found throughout the Teaching Guide, in Part Openers, Part Summaries, and Chapter Lessons. These activities cover a variety of content standard-related topics.

Also, developed specially for *A History of US* are the Johns Hopkins Team Learning Activities, which correlate to Part-wide themes and use cooperative learning models developed by Johns Hopkins University's Talent Development Middle School Program. (For more on these activities and how to use them, see page 21.) Also published by Oxford University Press, a complete curriculum, based on Team Learning Activities for *A History of US* is available. For more information, log on to *www.oup.com*.

Whether projects and assignments are geared toward solidifying understanding of the text or enriching connections with other disciplines is up to you.

▶ **Assign individual work**
Many exercises from the Teaching Guide **Check Understanding** section can be used for individual homework assignments. Student Study Guide pages can be assigned for homework as well.

▶ **Encourage students to create history journals for a portfolio approach**
Student Study Guide pages can be removed from the book and kept in a binder with writing assignments, artwork, and notes from projects as an individual portfolio. This approach creates a history journal, which has many benefits. It can be worked on at home and brought into class for assessment or sharing. It is a student's very own journal, where personal creativity can find an outlet. It also keeps all work organized and in order. Both the Teaching Guide and Student Study Guide contain a variety of analytical and creative writing projects that can be addressed in the history journal.

▶ **Assess however and whenever you need to**
This Teaching Guide contains the following assessment tools: cumulative, synthesis-based project ideas at the end of each Part, wrap-up tests, and scoring rubrics.

RUBRICS

At the back of this Teaching Guide you will find four reproducible rubric pages.

1. The Scoring Rubric page explains the evaluation categories. You may wish to go over and discuss each of these categories and points with your students.

2. A shortened handout version of the Scoring Rubric page has been included, with explanations of the categories and room for comments.

3. A student self-scoring rubric has been included. Use it to prompt your students to describe and evaluate both their work and participation in group projects.

4. A library/media center research log has also been included. Use this rubric as an aid to student research. It will help them plan and brainstorm research methods, record results, and evaluate their sources.

ASSESSMENT OPPORTUNITIES

Part Summaries were written specifically to give assessment ideas. They do this in two ways:

1. They refer to Part Check-Ups—reproducible tests at the back of the Teaching Guide that combine multiple choice, short answer, and an essay question to present a comprehensive assessment that covers the chapters in each Part.

2. They contains additional essay questions for alternate assessment as well as numerous project ideas. Projects can be assessed using the scoring rubrics at the back of the Teaching Guide.

ANSWER KEYS

An answer key at the back of the Teaching Guide contains answers for Part Check-Ups, Resource Pages, and Student Study Guide activities.

STUDENT STUDY GUIDE: KEY FEATURES

The Student Study Guide complements the activities in the Teaching Guide with exercises that build a context for the reading and strengthen analysis skills. Many activities encourage informal small group or family participation. In addition, the following features make it an effective teaching tool:

FLEXIBILITY

You can use the Study Guide in the classroom, with individuals or small groups, or send it home for homework. You can distribute the entire guide to students; however, the pages are perforated so you can remove and distribute only the pertinent lessons.

A page on reports and special projects in the front of the Study Guide directs students to the "More Books to Read" resource in the student edition. This feature gives students general guidance on doing research and devising independent study projects of their own.

FACSIMILE SPREAD

The Study Guide begins with a facsimile spread from the Student Edition. This spread gives reading strategies and highlights key features: captions, primary sources, sidebars, headings, etymologies. The spread supplies the contextualization students need to fully understand the material.

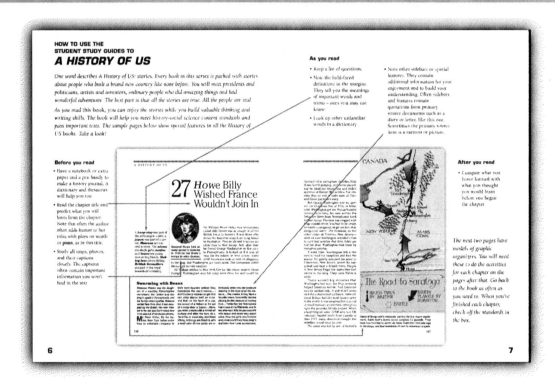

PORTFOLIO APPROACH

The Study Guide pages are three-hole-punched so they can be integrated with notebook paper in a looseleaf binder. This history journal or portfolio can become both a record of content mastery and an outlet for each student's unique creative expression. Responding to prompts, students can write poetry or songs, plays and character sketches, create storyboards or cartoons, or construct multi-layered timelines.

The portfolio approach gives students unlimited opportunities for practice in areas that need strengthening. And the Study Guide pages in the portfolio make a valuable assessment tool for you. It is an ongoing record of performance that can be reviewed and graded periodically.

GRAPHIC ORGANIZERS

This feature contains reduced models of seven graphic organizers referenced frequently in the guide. Using these devices will help students organize the material so it is more accessible. [Full-size reproducibles of each graphic organizer are provided at the back of this Teaching Guide.] These graphic organizers include: outline, main idea map, K-W-L chart (What I Know, What I Want to Know, What I Learned), Venn diagram, timeline, sequence of events chart, and t-chart.

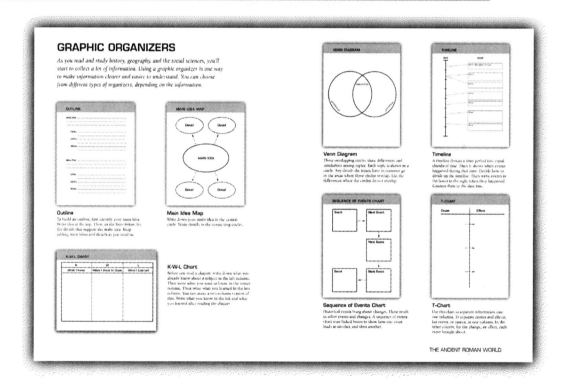

Each chapter lesson is designed to draw students into the subject matter. Recurring features and exercises challenge their knowledge and allow them to practice valuable analysis skills. Activities in the Teaching Guide and Student Study Guide complement but do not duplicate each other. Together they offer a wide range of class work, group projects, and opportunities for further study and assessment that can be tailored to all ability levels.

CHAPTER SUMMARY
briefly reviews big ideas from the chapter.

ACCESS
makes content accessible to students of all levels by incorporating graphic organizers into note taking.

WRITING
gives students writing suggestions drawn from the material. A writing assignment may stem from a vocabulary word, a historical event, a person, or a reading of a primary source. The assignment can take any number of forms: newspaper article, letter, short essay, a scene with dialogue, a diary entry.

CHAPTER 2

ABOUT BEING A PRESIDENT

SUMMARY *George Washington chose advisers to help him run the country.*

ACCESS

Have you ever tried to do a really hard job by yourself? Hard jobs are usually easier when you get people to help. President Washington could not run the country by himself. He needed advisers to assist him. Copy the main idea map from page 8 into your history journal. In the largest circle, put Washington's name. In each of the smaller circles, write the name of one of the people who helped Washington govern the nation. Below each name, write the job that the person had.

WORD BANK   precedent   executive   legislative   judicial   cabinet   dictatorship

Choose words from the word bank to complete the sentences. One word is not used at all.

1. The _____ branch includes the nation's courts.

2. A government that is run by an all-powerful leader is called a _____.

3. The president is the head of the _____ branch.

4. Washington chose Henry Knox to serve in his _____.

5. Congress is also called the _____ branch.

WORD PLAY

In the dictionary, look up the word you did not use. Write a sentence using that word.

_____

WITH A PARENT OR PARTNER

The United States has a three-branch government. Write the name of each branch at the top of a piece of paper. Below each name, write five words that relate to that particular branch of government. Ask a parent or partner to do the same. Then read your lists to each other.

WORKING WITH PRIMARY SOURCES

In 1792 Dr. Benjamin Rush wrote this about a hot air balloon flight by Jean-Pierre François Blanchard:

> For some time days past the conversation in our city has turned wholly upon Mr. Blanchard's late Aerial Voyage. It was truly a sublime sight. Every faculty of the mind was seized, expanded and captivated by it, 40,000 people concentrating their eyes and thoughts at the same instant, upon the same object, and all deriving nearly the same degree of pleasure from it.

1. How did Benjamin Rush feel about Blanchard's flight?

2. How did the people of Philadelphia feel about Blanchard's flight?

WRITING

Imagine that you are in Philadelphia watching Blanchard's flight. In your history journal, write a letter to a friend describing the event in your own words.

12   CHAPTER 2

CHAPTER 3

THE PARTIES BEGIN

SUMMARY *Alexander Hamilton and Thomas Jefferson had different ideas about what was best for the country. Their disagreements led to America's first party system.*

ACCESS

What is a political party? How many political parties can you think of? When George Washington took office, the United States did not have any political parties. He thought they caused conflict. Copy the main idea map from page 8 into your history journal. In the largest circle, put *Hamilton and Jefferson's Disagreements*. As you read the chapter, write an issue they disagreed about in each of the smaller circles.

WORD BANK

Federalist   liberal   credit   interest   Democratic-Republican   capitalist   collateral   invest   conservative   capital   bond   free enterprise system

Choose words from the word bank to complete the sentences. One word is not used at all.

1. Thomas Jefferson was the leader of the _____ party.

2. If you borrow money, you must pay _____.

3. A capitalist system is sometimes called a _____.

4. A _____ favors civil liberties, democratic reforms and the use of governmental power to promote social progress.

5. The _____ party consisted of Alexander Hamilton's supporters.

6. When people get a loan, sometimes they must provide _____.

7. A _____ is a written promise to pay back a loan.

8. Many farmers and solders decided to _____ in the new U.S. government.

9. A _____ is someone who is reluctant to make changes.

10. Another word for borrowing power is _____.

11. _____ is money, or any goods or assets that can be turned into money.

WORD PLAY

Identify two of the above terms that have similar meanings. Next identify two of the above terms that have opposite meanings. Write your answers below.

_____

CRITICAL THINKING COMPARE AND CONTRAST

The phrases below describe Alexander Hamilton and Thomas Jefferson. In your history journal, copy the Venn Diagram on page 9. Write *Hamilton* above one circle and *Jefferson* above the other circle. The phrases that apply to only one person go in that person's circle. The phrases that apply to both go in the area where the two circles connect.

wanted a free education amendment	had faith in ordinary people	fought for freedom of the press
concerned about balancing liberty and power	feared the masses	encouraged business and industry
wanted the government to pay off its debt	headed a major political party	
wanted aristocratic leaders to govern	feared a powerful government	

WORKING WITH PRIMARY SOURCES

Stephen Vincent Benét wrote a poem about one of the Founding Fathers.

He could handle the Nation's dollars | And scratch like a wildcat, too.
With a magic that's known to few, | And he yoked the States together
He could talk with the wits and scholars | With a yoke that is strong and stout.

Who is the subject of the poem? Which lines reveal the person's identity? Circle your answers in the poem.

THE NEW NATION   **13**

WORD BANK
reinforces key vocabulary from the student book and Teaching Guide.

CRITICAL THINKING
exercises draw on such thinking skills as establishing cause and effect, making inferences, drawing conclusions, determining sequence of events, comparing and contrasting, identifying main ideas and details, and other analytical process.

WORKING WITH PRIMARY SOURCES
invites students to read primary sources closely. Exercises include answering comprehension questions, evaluating point of view, and writing.

Strategic Methods for Content Learning

READING HISTORY
A PRACTICAL GUIDE TO IMPROVING LITERACY

JANET ALLEN
with Christine Landaker

Enhancing reading skills and learning history are inextricably linked. Students for whom reading is a challenge have difficulty immersing themselves in books and in historical narratives. With these students, improving literacy becomes crucial for teaching history.

Especially with struggling readers and English-language learners, comprehending the text is the first (and often most difficult) step toward engaging the story. *Reading History: A Practical Guide to Improving Literacy*, by Dr. Janet Allen, was written specifically to address teaching history to these students. *Reading History* is a book of instructional strategies for "building meaningful background knowledge that will support reading, writing, and research."

The instructional strategies in *Reading History* are modular components that can be understood with a minimum of instruction and can be applied easily as pre- and post-reading and writing activities. The Wordstorming and List-Group-Label exercises below are two examples of the simple and effective activities that can be the difference between giving information and building background that helps to improve literacy.

Dr. Allen and colleague Christine Landaker used *A History of US* to help create and illustrate the activities in *Reading History*, and examples from *A History of US* appear throughout the book, dovetailing the two books into a single, comprehensive, and successful literacy-based History curriculum.

From Reading History

WORDSTORMING
1. Ask students to write down all the words they can think of related to a given word (concept, theme, target word).

2. When students have exhausted their contributions, help them add to their individual lists by giving some specific directions.
   Can you think of words that describe someone without _____?
   Can you think of words that would show what someone might see, hear, feel, touch, smell in a situation filled with _____?

3. Ask students to group and label their words.

4. Add any words you think should be included and ask students to put them in the right group.

LIST-GROUP-LABEL
1. List all of the words you can think of related to _____ (major concept of text).

2. Group words that you have listed by words that have something in common.

3. Once words are grouped, decide on a label for each group.

USING THE JOHNS HOPKINS TEAM LEARNING ACTIVITIES

JOHNS HOPKINS
U N I V E R S I T Y

The Talent Development Middle School Program at Johns Hopkins University is a project of the Center for the Social Organization of Schools (CSOS). *A History of US* is the core of the American history curriculum in this whole-school reform effort. Oxford University Press proudly includes in this Teaching Guide selected lessons developed by Susan Dangel and Maria Gariott at the Talent Development Middle School Program.

You will find one Johns Hopkins Team Learning Activity at the end of each Part in this Teaching Guide. Keyed to appropriate chapters, the Team Learning Activity provides an opportunity to use cooperative learning models based on *A History of US*.

Each Activity begins with a Focus Activity that introduces the lesson, engages students, and draws on students' prior knowledge.

The heart of the lesson is a Team Learning Activity. In teams, students investigate lesson content, solve problems, use information for a purpose, and apply the tools of the historian.

Within the Student Team Learning Activity, the following techniques and strategies may be employed:

▶ Brainstorming: Students generate as many ideas as possible within a set time, before discussing and evaluating them.

▶ Roundtable: A brainstorming technique in which each team member contributes ideas on one sheet of paper and passes it to the next student. In Simultaneous Roundtable, more than one sheet is passed at the same time.

▶ Round Robin: An oral form of brainstorming in which one team member at a time states an idea.

▶ Think-Pair-Share: Students think about content or consider a question, then share their responses with a partner. In Think-Team-Share, students think through the prompt on their own and then share as a team.

▶ Partner Read: Students share a reading assignment with a partner.

▶ Timed Telling: A student or team is given a fixed time to share information, opinions, or results with the class.

▶ Team Investigation: Working in teams, students search and analyze the text, primary source materials, or other resource materials; draw conclusions; and make connections.

▶ Jigsaw: Within each team, students select or are assigned specific questions or subjects on which to become experts. Experts meet and investigate in Expert Teams, then regroup in their original teams to report out their findings.

▶ Numbered Heads: Each team member is assigned a number—1, 2, 3, and so on. Team members work together on the team learning activity. The teacher selects one number and asks the person with that number in each team to report the team response.

IMPROVING LITERACY WITH A HISTORY OF US

PROVIDING ACCESS

The books in this series are written in a lively, narrative style to inspire a love of reading. English language learners and struggling readers are given special consideration within the program's exercises and activities. And students who love to read and learn will also benefit from the program's rich and varied material. Following are expert strategies to make sure each and every student gets the most out of the subjects you will teach through *A History of US*.

ADVANCED LEARNERS

Every classroom has students who finish the required assignments and then want additional challenges. Fortunately, the very nature of history and social science offers a wide range of opportunities for students to explore topics in greater depth. Encourage them to come up with their own ideas for an additional assignment. Determine the final product, its presentation, and a timeline for completion.

Research

Students can develop in-depth understanding through seeking information, exploring ideas, asking and answering questions, making judgments, considering points of view, and evaluating actions and events. They will need access to a wide range of resource materials: the Internet, maps, encyclopedias, trade books, magazines, dictionaries, artifacts, newspapers, museum catalogues, brochures, and the library. See the "More Books to Read" section at the end of the Student Edition for good jumping-off points.

Projects

You can encourage students to capitalize on their strengths as learners (visual, verbal, kinesthetic, or musical) or to try a new way of responding. Students can prepare a debate or write a persuasive paper, play, skit, poem, song, dance, game, puzzle, or biography. They can create an alphabet book on the topic, film a video, do a book talk, or illustrate a book. They can render charts, graphs, or other visual representations. Allow for creativity and support students' thinking.

ENGLISH LANGUAGE LEARNERS

For English learners to achieve academic success, the instructional considerations for teachers include two mandates:

▶ Help them attain grade level, content area knowledge, and academic language.
▶ Provide for the development of English language proficiency.

To accomplish these goals, you should plan lessons that reflect the student's level of English proficiency. Students progress through five developmental levels as they increase in language proficiency:

▶ Beginning and Early Intermediate (grade level material will be mostly incomprehensible, students need a great deal of teacher support)
▶ Intermediate (grade level work will be a challenge)
▶ Early Advanced and Advanced (close to grade level reading and writing, students continue to need support)

Tap Prior Knowledge

What students know about the topic will help determine your next steps for instruction. Using K-W-L charts, brainstorming, and making lists are ways to find out what they know. English learners bring a rich cultural diversity into the classroom. By sharing what they know, students can connect their knowledge and experiences to the course.

Set the Context

Use different tools to make new information understandable. These can be images, artifacts, maps, timelines, illustrations, charts, videos, or graphic organizers. Techniques such as role-playing and story-boarding can also be helpful. Speak in shorter sentences, with careful enunciation, expanded explanations, repetitions, and paraphrasing. Use fewer idiomatic expressions.

Show—Don't Just Tell

English learners often get lost as they listen to directions, explanations, lectures, and discussions. By showing students what is expected, you can help them participate more fully in classroom activities. Students need to be shown how to use the graphic organizers in the student study guide, as well as other blackline masters for note-taking and practice. An overhead transparency with whole or small groups is also effective.

Use the Text

Because of unfamiliar words, students will need help with understanding. Teach them to preview the chapter using text features (headings, bold print, sidebars, italics). See the suggestions in the facsimile of the Student Edition, shown on pages 6–7 of the Student Study Guide. Show students organizing structures such as cause and effect or comparing and contrasting. Have students read to each other in pairs. Help them create word banks, charts, and graphic organizers. Discuss the main idea after reading.

Check for Understanding

Rather than simply ask students if they understand, stop frequently and ask them to paraphrase or expand on what you just said. Such techniques will give you a much clearer assessment of their understanding.

Provide for Interaction

As students interact with the information and speak their thoughts, their content knowledge and academic language skills improve. Increase interaction in the classroom through cooperative learning, small group work, and partner share. By working and talking with others, students can practice asking and answering questions.

Use Appropriate Assessment

When modifying the instruction, you will also need to modify the assessment. Multiple choice, true and false, and other criterion reference tests are suitable, but consider changing test format and structure. English learners are constantly improving their language proficiency in their oral and written responses, but they are often grammatically incorrect. Remember to be thoughtful and fair about giving students credit for their content knowledge and use of academic language, even if their English isn't perfect.

STRUGGLING READERS

Some students struggle to understand the information presented in a textbook. The following strategies for content-area reading can help students improve their ability to make comparisons, sequence events, determine importance, summarize, evaluate, synthesize, analyze, and solve problems.

Build Knowledge of Genre

Both fiction and narrative nonfiction genres are incorporated into *A History of US*. This combination of genres makes the text interesting and engaging. But teachers must be sure students can identify and use the organizational structures of both genres.

The textbook has a wealth of the text features of nonfiction: bold and italic print, sidebars, headings and subheadings, labels, captions, and "signal words" such as first, next, and finally. Teaching these organizational structures and text features is essential for struggling readers.

Fiction

Each chapter is a story

Setting: historical time and place

Characters: historical figures

Plot: problems, roadblocks, and resolutions

Non-Fiction

Content: historical information

Organizational structure: cause/effect, sequence of events, problem/solution

Other features: maps, timelines, sidebars, photographs, primary sources

Build Background

Having background information about a topic makes reading about it so much easier. When students lack background information, teachers can preteach or "front load" concepts and vocabulary, using a variety of instructional techniques. Conduct a "chapter or bookwalk," looking at titles, headings, and other text features to develop a big picture of the content. Focus in new vocabulary words during the "walk" and create a word bank with illustrations for future reference. Read aloud key passages and discuss the meaning. Focus on the timeline and maps to help students develop a sense of time and place. Show a video, go to a website, and have trade books and magazines on the topic available for student exploration.

Comprehension Strategies

While reading, successful readers are predicting, making connections, monitoring, visualizing, questioning, inferring, and summarizing. Struggling readers have a harder time with these "in the head" processes. The following strategies will help these students construct meaning from the text until they are able to do it on their own.

Predict

Before reading, conduct a picture and text feature "tour" of the chapter to make predictions. Ask students if they remember if this has ever happened before, to predict what might happen this time.

Make Connections

Help students relate content to their background (text to text, text to self, and text to the world).

Monitor And Confirm

Encourage students to stop reading when they come across an unknown word, phrase, or concept. In their notebooks, have them make a note of text they don't understand and ask for clarification or figure it out. While this activity slows down reading at first, it is effective in improving skills over time.

Visualize

Students benefit from imagining the events described in a story. Sketching scenes, story-boarding, role-playing, and looking for sensory details all help students with this strategy.

Infer

Help students look beyond the literal meaning of a text to understand deeper meanings. Graphic organizers and discussions provide opportunities to broaden their understanding. Looking closely at the "why" of historical events helps students infer.

Question And Discuss

Have students jot down their questions as they read, and then share them during discussions. Or have students come up with the type of questions they think a teacher would ask. Over time students will develop more complex inferential questions, which lead to group discussions. Questioning and discussing also helps students see ideas from multiple perspectives and draw conclusions, both critical skills for understanding history.

Determine Importance

Teach students how to decide what is most important from all the facts and details in nonfiction. After reading for an overall understanding, they can go back to highlight important ideas, words, and phrases. Clues for determining importance include bold or italic print, signal words, and other text features. A graphic organizer such as a main idea map also helps.

Teach and Practice Decoding Strategies

Rather than simply defining an unfamiliar word, teach struggling readers decoding strategies: have them look at the prefix, suffix, and root to help figure out the new word, look for words they know within the word, use the context for clues, and read further or reread.

— Cheryl A. Caldera, M.A.
Literacy Coach

TEACHING STRATEGIES FOR *WAR, TERRIBLE WAR*

INTRODUCING BOOK SIX

Part 1: A Terrible Remedy   1830–1861
Part 2: A Growing Crisis   1809–1859
Part 3: The South Secedes   1861–1862
Part 4: A House Divided   1861–1865
Part 5: Ordeal by Fire   1861–1863
Part 6: An End—And a Beginning)   1864–1865

New Year's Day, Emancipation Day, was a glorious one for us....Our hearts were filled with an exceeding great gladness; for although the government had left much undone, we knew that Freedom was surely born in our land that day. It seemed too glorious a good to realize, this beginning of the great work we had so longed for and prayed for...."Forever free! Forever free!"—those magical words in the President's Proclamation were constantly singing themselves in my soul.

General Robert E. Lee

For 24-year-old Charlotte Forten, the sound of a Union officer reading aloud the Emancipation Proclamation would remain etched in her memory. So would the faces of the enslaved Africans that she had traveled to the South Carolina Sea Islands to teach. "It was a sight never to be forgotten," recalled Forten, "that crowd of happy black faces from which the shadow of Slavery had forever passed."

As Forten accurately noted, the Emancipation Proclamation "left much undone." It applied only to lands under Confederate control. It left slavery untouched in loyal border states and in cities or counties already occupied by Union troops. But, as a war measure, it was without precedent. In issuing this executive order, Abraham Lincoln committed the Union to abolition. He also laid the groundwork for backing a more radical action a year and a half later. In June 1864, Lincoln instructed the chairman of the Republican Party to "put into the platform as a keystone, the amendment of the Constitution abolishing and prohibiting slavery forever."

General Ulysses S. Grant

The abolition of slavery was a long time in coming. Even as colonists boldly proclaimed their own liberty, they edited references to slavery out of the Declaration of Independence. Muttered a sullen Thomas Jefferson: "Nothing is more certainly written than that these people [enslaved Africans] are to be free." But repeated compromises all but institutionalized slavery. Compromise allowed veiled references to slavery to creep into the Constitution. Compromise drew artificial political boundaries that allowed slavery to spread outside the South. Even as the abolitionist movement spawned new political debate, able political leaders in both North and South worked to prevent slavery from breaking up the Union. As late as 1858, Jefferson Davis declared: "This great country will continue united....[The United States] is my country and to the innermost fibers of my heart I love it all, and every part."

Why then did civil war come to the United States? In a land founded upon the principles of liberty, slavery simply was an issue that could not be compromised forever. The conflict over slavery was too fundamental. Maintaining or abolishing it called up too many political, economic, and social issues. The debate triggered too many intense emotions on each side. And the North and South considered the issue too important for the nation's future to ignore. In 1860, Abraham Lincoln put the matter in its most basic terms in a conversation with his old friend, Alexander Stephens of Georgia. Said Lincoln: "You think that slavery is *right* and ought to be extended; while we think it

Confederate volunteers

is *wrong* and ought to be restricted. That I suppose is the rub."

The extension of slavery into the territories made conflict impossible to avoid. A rapid-fire series of events intensified Southern fears: publication of *Uncle Tom's Cabin*, Northern disregard of the Fugitive Slave Law, John Brown's raid on Harper's Ferry, and election in 1860 of an antislavery President. Starting with South Carolina, 11 states marched out of the Union.

Although slavery lay at the root of the Civil War, neither side squarely addressed the issue at first. Confederates talked of states' rights and liberty to chart their own course. They called the conflict a "revolution" and compared themselves to the Patriots of 1776. Abraham Lincoln, the voice of constant moderation, talked of Union and the need to preserve "government of the people, by the people, for the people." He saw the Civil War as a test of free, democratic government. Could a republic put down a rebellion without resorting to tyranny in the aftermath? Lincoln thought it could, and he committed the nation's youth to a struggle they could understand. Only with caution did Lincoln interject abolition into the Northern war aims. Only when he knew the North was ready to support this most revolutionary step—fighting for the rights of people of color—and only after the much sought-after Union "victory" at Antietam in 1862, did he announce the Emancipation Proclamation.

However, Lincoln knew that no proclamation by itself would end slavery and win the war. The South still had tens of thousands of soldiers under arms, led by superior generals. As the war dragged on, Lincoln had to contend not only with weak military leadership, but also with a public that questioned whether the costs of the war were worth it. But in the first week of July 1863, the North won two decisive victories: On July 3, Union forces won the battle of Gettysburg, ending Confederate hopes of winning the war by invading the North. A day later, the Southern stronghold of Vicksburg on the Mississippi fell to General Ulysses S. Grant, giving control of that waterway to the North and splitting the Confederacy in two.

Southerners, however, did not surrender easily. For nearly two more years the battles raged. Even as Sherman was ravaging Georgia and the Carolinas, Lee held his outnumbered Army of Northern Virginia together in the face of Grant's relentless assaults. Then, on April 2, 1865, Grant forced Lee's ragged, half-starved armies to abandon their lines around the Confederate capital of Richmond.

A week later, on April 9, the nation's most destructive war

ended in a handshake between Grant and Lee. When Lee surrendered, the Confederacy and slavery collapsed. So did extreme forms of the states' rights controversy. But two crucial questions remained unresolved: On what terms would the South return to the Union? And more importantly, what role would African Americans play in the nation?

For answers to these questions, people looked to the compassionate President who promised "malice toward none." But expectation turned to tragedy when an assassin's bullet ended Lincoln's life. "The whole world bowed their heads in grief when Abraham Lincoln died," said Elizabeth Keckley, once enslaved herself. Confederate General George Pickett mourned, "The South has lost her best friend and protector in this her direst hour of need." The fate of the nation now passed into the hands of a President less skilled at controlling the fiery passions of a postwar Congress.

Book Six traces the path from Fort Sumter to Appomattox Court House. Each of the six parts recommended for teaching this book serves as a "roadmarker" on this journey.

President Lincoln meets General McClellan

Pickett's charge, Battle of Gettysburg

INTRODUCING THE BOOK WITH PROJECTS AND ACTIVITIES

INTRODUCING THE BIG IDEAS

Conflict and liberty are the two Big Ideas in *War, Terrible War* (Book Six of *A History of US*). They provide the conceptual framework that holds together the 31 chapters and hundreds of individual stories in this volume of *A History of US.*

Introducing your students to these concepts at the beginning of the book will help them to put together the reasons Americans became caught up in a civil war—a war that claimed over 600,000 lives. You might introduce the idea of conflict by writing the title of this book—*War, Terrible War*—on the chalkboard. Students will undoubtedly connect conflict to the physical acts of war. But they might not think about the personal conflicts that develop during a civil war. First, be sure that students understand the meaning of *civil* (relating to or of the community or group; thus, a civil war is one within a group). Ask students why a civil war is one of the worst kinds of war in which a people can engage.

Next, cite the number of Americans who died in the Civil War. To help students appreciate the reasons that motivated so many people to sacrifice their lives, read aloud this statement from *The Killer Angels* by Michael Shaara: "The American fights for mankind, for freedom; for the people, not the land." Ask students what war in history had already proven this. *(the American Revolution)* Encourage them to think about the freedoms for which Americans might have been willing to fight in the mid-1800s. To help students, suggest they recall what they have learned about the different ways that people struggled for equality in early American history.

FOCUSING ON LITERACY

SETTING THE CONTEXT
You can set a context for reading by referring students to the quote by George Mason on page 12 of Book Six. Ask students what fate Mason predicted for the nation. *(national calamities)* Why? *(because of the practice of slavery)* Focus on the words *an inevitable chain of causes and effects.* Brainstorm with students some of the links in this causal chain. In other words, what conflicts had erupted over slavery before? What was the effect of each conflict? You may want to suggest that students skim through the chronologies at the end of previous books in the series. Ask students to speculate on whether this chain can be broken only by war. Why?

CHARTING CAUSE AND EFFECT
Of particular importance in Book Six are the cause-and-effect relationships. Some of the teaching suggestions ask students to identify underlying and immediate causes of the war. Students are also asked to identify short- and long-term effects of the war. These activities will help students to answer a question raised by the author: What did the war accomplish? (The answer, as students will see, is the expansion of liberty.) To help students organize their understanding of the most destructive war in our history, encourage them to create graphic organizers for analyzing cause and effect. Have students create flow charts or other

cause-and-effect diagrams in their notebooks or on a bulletin board on which they can diagram the causes and effects of significant Civil War events. You might have them graphically differentiate between underlying and immediate causes, or use different-length arrows to mark short- and long-term effects. For example, slavery and John Brown's raid were both causes of the war, but the former was an underlying cause while the latter was immediate. The Battle of Gettysburg—the military turning point of the war—had relatively short-term impact, whereas the impact of the Emancipation Proclamation is still being felt today.

READING FURTHER

On page 160 of Book Six, Joy Hakim notes that some 50,000 books have been published on the Civil War. Encourage students to bring in Civil War books from home or from the school or community library. They can also write brief reviews of each book, or flag interesting passages and pictures for other students to look at. You may want to have groups of students locate different types of materials: biographies, diaries, illustrated histories, and so on. One way to hook students is to explain that the Civil War was one of the first wars to be widely photographed. Seeing some of these photos (such as the thousands in the Mathew Brady collection) often begins a lifelong interest in the war.

ONGOING PROJECTS

The following activities bridge the six parts in *War, Terrible War.*

USING TIME LINES

Author Joy Hakim advises that a sense of chronology, rather than memorized dates, is what matters for students. Various kinds of time lines are invaluable aids in building this understanding of historical sequence.

The author helps set a framework in time by providing a chronology at the end of each of the ten books in this series. A class time line, started at the beginning of the year, will help students place each segment of their study in sequence. You and your students can create such a time line with long sheets of butcher paper. Connected sheets of computer paper, calculator paper, or even clothesline also work well. Invite the class to illustrate the time lines with drawings, maps, and photocopied illustrations.

Students also can create smaller class and personal time lines that focus on the main block of time covered in Book Six.

Assessment/Sequencing When students have completed the class and individual time lines, have them use events on the time line to evaluate and revise their cause-and-effect charts. Encourage students to organize events under the following headings: *Underlying Causes, Immediate Causes, Short-Term Effects, Long-Term Effects.* Ask students if any of the causes of the Civil War were still present at the end of the war. (*Slavery was abolished, but the issue of states' rights—how individual states relate to the federal government—still stirs debate.*)

USING THE RUBRICS

To assess these writing assignments, group projects, and activities, scoring rubrics have been provided at the back to this Teaching Guide. Be sure to explain the rubrics to your students.

REPRODUCIBLE MAPS

The Student Study Guides for this book include blank maps for projects included in the Study Guide. You may also use these blank maps for additional activities.

USING MAPS

Map activities are essential to understanding the Civil War. By mapping regions, battles, and events for themselves, students can visually organize the complex details of this period. Included in this guide and the Student Study Guides are several blank/reproducible maps to use for this purpose. On these maps, locations of major cities are marked by locator dots, and students can correlate these dots to the United States political map in the Atlas section of their book.

War Room Map Activity   Activities throughout this guide will direct students to mark battle sites, tactics, and movements to create a "Civil War Room map," similar to the war room map charting the events in the Revolutionary War in Book 3. Found in chapter lessons under Geography Connections, the Civil War Room map activity will list ongoing additions to this cumulative map. You can reinforce map reading skills by having students locate important sites by the map coordinates provided, by giving directions from the nearest locator dot, or by referring to maps in their books. Use the reproducible map provided and also have students make wall sized maps in groups. In addition, you may wish to gather relief or military maps of specific battle sites, such as Bull Run or Antietam, to help students understand the important of geography and terrain in the Civil War.

WRITING HISTORY

The author hopes that students will become historians in their own way. She encourages them to retell and add to the stories in each book in *A History of US.* One way to accomplish this is to ask students to set up a separate section in their history journal in which they write their own history books. After finishing each chapter, give students time to write their own account of the events. (Students may want to dig deeper into the past or illustrate their stories with pictures.) Point out that Joy Hakim often suggests ideas for further investigation. From time to time, ask volunteers to share their histories with the class.

Assessment/Editing Historical Writing   When students have finished their own histories for Book Six, have them exchange them with other students. Challenge students to pick one or two chapters in their classmate's book for editing. Students can list on a separate sheet of paper suggestions for needed clarifications or other improvements. They should also note well-written or especially interesting selections. Student editors should meet with authors to discuss the changes. After authors have revised their work, ask volunteers to read their chapters aloud. Encourage them to note any editorial tips that helped improve their writing.

THE BIG IDEAS

When abolitionist Frederick Douglass heard of the Confederate attack on Fort Sumter, he exclaimed:

God be praised! The slaveholders have saved our cause. They have exposed the throat of slavery to the keen knife of liberty.

Part 1 introduces the two closely related issues that divided the nation in 1860—states' rights and slavery. Slavery was the beast that lurked just below the surface. However, it was the storm over states' rights that led to the creation of the Confederacy and Lincoln's resolve not to let a minority break up the Union. The conflict began as a spectator event at Fort Sumter and then Bull Run, but picnic grounds quickly became killing fields and the terrible war had begun.

PART 1

A TERRIBLE REMEDY

PREFACE I–CHAPTER 2
Preface I: Dinner at Brown's Hotel 9
Preface II: A Divided Nation 11
1   Americans Fighting Americans 14
2   The War Begins 17

INTRODUCING PART 1

SETTING GOALS

Write these terms on the chalkboard: *states' rights, civil war,* and *slavery,* and discuss the meaning of each. Explain that two of these were causes, and one was an effect, and have students identify which was which. *(Causes: states' rights, slavery; effect: civil war. Students should understand that most wars are the result of a chain of events. Even a long war may be only the final chapter in a generations-old struggle.)*

To set goals for Part 1, tell students that they will
• explain why states' rights divided the country.
• summarize how the expansion of slavery divided the nation.
• compare and contrast the North's and the South's view on secession.
• understand how the Battle of Bull Run changed expectations about the war.

SETTING A CONTEXT FOR READING
Thinking About the Big Ideas   To illustrate the conflict between slavery and American ideals, refer students to page 11 of Book Six and focus on the enslaved man in the photo to the right. Then read aloud the quotation from the Declaration of Independence. Have students write down any thoughts or feelings they have. Request volunteers to share their reactions with the class. Next, ask students to write a new caption for the photo, using the words *conflict* and *liberty*.

Identifying a Root Cause   Historians have debated the primary cause of the Civil War—states' rights and slavery being the most prominent. Ask students if they think the war would have occurred if either of these issues had not been present. Help students understand that if slavery did not exist in the United States, states' rights probably would not have become such an important issue.

SETTING A CONTEXT IN SPACE AND TIME

Using Maps   Have students refer to the map of the United States in the Atlas in their book. Ask students to show the advance of the division between free and slave states, starting from the Missouri Compromise and continuing through the Compromise of 1850 and the Kansas-Nebraska Act. Discuss how despite the compromises, the conflict over slavery simply moved westward as the country grew.

Understanding the Closeness of the Past   Although the Civil War may seem like ancient history to students, it occurred only four generations ago. Students' great-great-grandparents (their grandparents' grandparents) might have had a part in the war, if they lived in the United States. As recently as the 1950s, when some students' parents were children, there were still surviving veterans of the Union and Confederate armed forces. Students may want to do Internet research on Civil War veterans' organizations such as the Grand Army of the Republic and their members' activities.

PREFACE	1	DINNER AT BROWN'S HOTEL
		PAGES 9-10

PREFACE	2	A DIVIDED NATION
		PAGES 11-13

1 Class Period

Chapter Summary

In 1830, the competing toasts of President Jackson and Vice President Calhoun foreshadowed the coming split in the country over states' rights. The other overarching issue was slavery, which most Americans seemed willing to ignore until the country's growth opened the question of whether the western lands would be free or slave.

Key Vocabulary

peculiar institution   states' rights   abolitionist

1. CONNECT

Call on volunteers to describe quickly some of the differences between the Northern and Southern states that were leading to war.

2. UNDERSTAND

1. Read Preface I. Discuss: How do the toasts of Jackson and Calhoun foreshadow civil war? (*Their toasts show that neither side would compromise on the issue of states' rights.*)
2. Read Preface II. Discuss: What economic, racial, and political issues were raised by slavery? (*Economic: provided a cheap source of labor for the South. Racial: created racial prejudice by enslaving people of color. Political: threatened to undermine the principles on which the nation was founded.*)

3. CHECK UNDERSTANDING

Writing   Have partners write short speeches supporting either side of the states' rights argument.

Thinking About the Chapter (Hypothesizing)   Discuss what the situation would be like for the Northern and Southern states if the Union had split apart into two separate countries. How would their economies be affected? Their foreign relations? Would the two countries have existed peacefully, or would they eventually have gone to war with each other?

NOTE TO THE TEACHER

When you see the instruction "Read..." you can interpret it in any way that fits the lesson you are creating for your students. For example, you may read aloud to the class or to small groups, you may have volunteers read aloud, or you may have the class read silently.

READING NONFICTION

Analyzing Text Features

Have students identify the text features found in the prefaces, including titles, sidebar quotations, italicized quotations, sidebars that explain vocabulary or concepts, and captions for photographs, drawings, or cartoons. Explain that the sidebars may be read first, as a way of previewing the text. Then ask: How do the sidebars create interest in the text? (*by attracting interest visually as well as by giving interesting nuggets of information*)

READING NONFICTION

Analyzing Graphic Devices

Have students brainstorm ways that political cartoons express ideas. (*with humor, irony, exaggeration, innuendo, and images*) Have partners write a short explanation of each cartoon in the chapter, including an analysis of the most striking visual image in each.

NOTE FROM THE AUTHOR

Before the Civil War, Americans called our country "the Union" or "these [plural] United States." After the Civil War, we dropped that word union *and referred to ourselves as a nation and as "the [singular] United States."*

GEOGRAPHY CONNECTIONS

The author wants to know: Which were the old Southern states? Which Southern states were new? (*Students can use maps in the Atlas in their textbook to name the old states—those in the original 13 states, and the new states added by 1831.*)

LINKING DISCIPLINES

Art/Politics

Have students draw their own pro- or anti-secessionist cartoon, and present their work to the class.

HISTORY ARCHIVES

A History of US Sourcebook

#45, From John C. Calhoun, "*Proposal to Preserve the Union": Speech on the Compromise of 1850* (1850)

1 Class Period   **Homework: Student Study Guide p. 11**

Chapter Summary

All wars are terrible, but the worst are those fought within a nation. In the case of the United States, two great issues hung in the balance—the fate of republican government and the limits of liberty.

Key Vocabulary

Rebel   secede   Yankee

1. CONNECT

Civil wars are all too common in history. Ask students to recall other instances of civil war that they know about, ancient or modern. Could a civil war ever break out in America today? Over what issue?

2. UNDERSTAND

1. Read the chapter. Discuss: Why does the author say that "neither side came out ahead" after the war? (*Students should mention the financial and human costs of the war.*)
2. Discuss: What were the positions of the Southerners and Northerners with respect to states' rights and slavery? (*Southerners: states had the right to leave the Union; black people are not equal to white people. Northerners: Southern states had no "just cause" to leave Union; slavery was wrong.*)

3. CHECK UNDERSTANDING

Writing   Have students write a one-paragraph letter from President Lincoln to the South Carolina legislature attempting to persuade the South Carolinians that secession was not the proper course to take. Students should include arguments against the doctrine of states' rights.

Thinking About the Chapter (Making Judgments)   Have students think back to the nation's founders. Do they think that people like Washington, Jefferson, Franklin, Adams, Randolph, or Henry considered that states might leave the Union when they wrote the Constitution?

2 THE WAR BEGINS

PAGES 17-22

1 Class Period   **Homework: Student Study Guide p. 11**

Chapter Summary

After Southerners captured Fort Sumter, soldiers on both sides confidently marched off to battle. One of the first casualties was the hope of a quick, glorious war. The bloodshed and chaos of the battle of Manassas (Bull Run) revealed the extent of the tragedy to come.

Key Vocabulary

gun bore   rebel yell

1. CONNECT

Ask students what people tend to do when there is a car crash or a house fire. (*They stop and watch the disaster.*) Explain that this was people's reactions to the early battles in the Civil War, too.

2. UNDERSTAND

1. Read page 17. Discuss: Why did both the North and the South believe they would win a quick victory? (*Both sides underestimated the other and were overconfident in their own abilities.*)
2. Read the rest of the chapter. Discuss: What factors did neither side take into account in their thinking about the war? (*Possible responses: armies' lack of experience; new, deadlier weapons; individual bravery and resolve*)

3. CHECK UNDERSTANDING

Writing   Have students imagine that they are reporters for either the *Charleston Mercury* or the *New York Tribune* covering the battle of Manassas (Bull Run). They should write a short report of the battle, create a headline for the story, and end with a prediction about the course of the war.

Thinking About the Chapter (Analyzing)   Have a volunteer read aloud the quotation from Bruce Catton (page 19), phrase by phrase. Ask students to specify details from the chapter supporting each of Catton's points.

READING NONFICTION

Analyzing Primary Sources

Discuss with students why the author includes so many eyewitness accounts. (*to show what people at the time thought, observed, and did*) Have students explain what the quotation from the *Charleston Mercury* on page 17 reveals about Southern attitudes about the war. (*It suggests that the attack on Fort Sumter is akin to the Boston Tea Party, linking the Southern cause to that of the American Revolution.*)

MEETING INDIVIDUAL NEEDS

Have visual learners examine the pictures of Confederate soldiers on pages 20–21. What do they reveal about Southern attitudes toward the war at this point? (*Southerners seemed excited and confident.*)

MORE ABOUT...

Jackson's Nickname

Historian Shelby Foote says that General Jackson was also called "Old Blue-light" by his soldiers because his eyes would light up during battle.

ACTIVITIES/JOHNS HOPKINS TEAM LEARNING

See the Student Team Learning Activity on TG page 32.

GEOGRAPHY CONNECTIONS

Civil War Room Activity

Have students begin the Civil War Room activity as described on TG page 26. Have them outline and mark Northern and Southern states. Have them locate and mark the following:

Fort Sumter	32°45'N 79°52'W
Manassas (Bull Run)	38°45'N 77°30'W

JOHNS HOPKINS TEAM LEARNING

WHY THEY FOUGHT

1 CLASS PERIOD

FOCUS ACTIVITY

1. Have students **Partner Read** the descriptions of Southern and Northern soldiers on page 17. One partner should read about the Southerners, the other about the Northerners.

2. Have partners use **Think-Pair-Share** to answer these questions: (a) Before the war started, what did the Southern and Northern soldiers think about each other? (b) What was the common attitude about the war?

3. Ask partners to **Predict** how the soldiers' attitudes and beliefs about each other and the war will change after the first battle.

STUDENT TEAM LEARNING ACTIVITY/IDENTIFYING REASONS FOR GOING TO WAR

1. Organize students into teams of four, and distribute Resource Page 2 (TG page 100).

2. Have teams use **Round Robin** to list reasons why they would go fight in a war.

3. Have teams form partnerships to read the quotations on Resource Page 2: one partnership reading the Northern quotations, one the Southern quotations. Ask partnerships to read, discuss, and categorize reasons that soldiers decided to fight in the Civil War. When they have finished, partnerships come together to review their work and compare and contrast the reasons for both sides in the war. Have them decide on general categories for the reasons, such as patriotism, protecting homes, states' rights, liberty, abolition of slavery, preserving the Union, and so on.

4. **Circulate and Monitor** to help students interpret more difficult passages. Encourage students with the thought that they are evaluating historical documents as professional historians do.

5. Use **Numbered Heads** for teams to share their categories. Through discussion, guide students to understand that the personal decision to fight was very complicated and often had little to do with the major aims of either side.

ASSESSMENT

Part 1 Check-Up   Use Check-Up 1 (TG page 93) to assess student learning in Part 1.

ALTERNATE ASSESSMENT
Ask students to write an essay answering one of the following questions, which link the Big Ideas across chapters.

1. Making Connections   What was the connection between the sectional conflicts of the 1830s and the outbreak of civil war in 1861? *(Students should conclude that the debate over slavery and states' rights hardened differences between North and South, making them irreconcilable.)*

2. Making Connections   What was the connection between western expansion and the Civil War? *(Students should discuss details of how the existence of new territories and states forced people to confront the issue of whether slavery would grow along with the nation.)*

DEBATING THE ISSUES
Use the topics below to stimulate debate.

1. Resolved   That the Confederate states had the right to secede from the Union. (To encourage debate, appoint students to speak for the Rebels and the Federals. Students might role play these historical figures: Alexander Hamilton, Patrick Henry, John C. Calhoun, Andrew Jackson, and Daniel Webster.)

2. Resolved   That the only course of action open to President Lincoln after the attack on Fort Sumter was to declare war on the Confederacy. You might organize this as a meeting of Lincoln's Cabinet. Students should take the role of economic, polical, legal, military, and moral advisers, as well as Lincoln. The group should consider the consequences of not declaring war as well as the consequences of declaring war.)

MAKING ETHICAL JUDGMENTS
The following activity asks students to consider issues of ethics.

The author mentions that for many years people who didn't like slavery kept quiet. She asks: "Was that wrong?" Put yourself in the shoes of a Northerner in the 1830s. You've just attended a rally of "troublemakers" called abolitionists. How would you react to the ideas? In what ways would they challenge your silence? Write a diary entry in which you describe your feelings about abolitionists, slavery, and what you think your future actions will be. (Encourage students to consider that wrongs are all around us today, yet we often do not get involved unless the situation affects us directly. We also tend to see those who challenge old ways as being "troublemakers" to be avoided.)

USING THE RUBRICS

To assess these writing assignments, group projects, and activities, scoring rubrics have been provided at the back of this Teaching Guide. Be sure to explain the rubrics to your students.

PROJECTS AND ACTIVITIES

Writing a Play   The author starts off the story of John Calhoun and Andrew Jackson (page 9 of Book Six) like a play. Have students work in groups and add dialogue and stage directions to complete the account. Students can fictionalize conversation, toasts, and add other people at the dinner, but comments should reflect opinions of the time. Request volunteers to perform the plays. As a follow-up activity, assign students to write reviews of one of the plays for a Northern or Southern newspaper in the 1830s.

Analyzing a Quote   New Yorker Frederick Law Olmsted traveled the South widely in the 1850s. Read aloud these remarks about slavery that he recorded:

Well, sir, I know slavery is wrong, and God'll put an end to it....[A]nd when the end does come, there'll be woe in the land. And, instead of preparing for it, and trying to make it as light as possible, we are doing nothing but make it worse and worse....I'd rather get out of these parts before it comes.

Ask students how this speaker feels about slavery. What future does he foresee when slavery is ended? Why might such a person support the Confederacy despite objections to slavery? (Lead students to see that a only a few white Southerners could propose alternative lives for themselves. Many non-slaveowning whites were terrified that any status they had in Southern society would be threatened with the end of slavery. And almost no Southern leaders could imagine a society where black people were free and equal to whites.)

Identifying the Issue   Read aloud or distribute copies of Lincoln's July 4, 1861, war message to Congress:

Our popular government has often been called an experiment....It is now [time] for...[us] to demonstrate to the world that those who can fairly carry an election can also suppress a rebellion;...that when ballots have fairly decided,...there can be no successful appeal back to bullets....Such will be a great lesson of peace: teaching men that what they cannot take by election, neither can they take by war.

Assign students to report Lincoln's war message in the form of a news story. The headline should identify the main issue addressed by Lincoln: the cause of war.

Contrasting Opinions   Have students imagine that they are members of a South Carolina regiment who were present at both the bombardment of Fort Sumter and the Battle of Menassas. Have them write short letters home describing their feelings after each battle and their opinion of what the rest of the war will be like.

Writing an Editorial   Read aloud the quote by Frederick Douglass on TG page 27. Then challenge students to use this remark to write an editorial on Fort Sumter that Douglass might have run in the *North Star*. The editorial might criticize Lincoln for not openly citing slavery in his war message to Congress. (See above quote.)

Summarizing Information   Challenge students to imagine they are reporters observing the battle of Manassas (Bull Run). At the end of the battle, they rush into a telegraph office in Washington, D.C., to cable news of the battle to their home office in either New York City or Charleston. Their messages must be 25 words or less. Assign students to boil down the conflict to its most essential points. Compare the messages sent to Charleston with those sent to New York City. How do they differ?

LOOKING AHEAD

Identifying Cause and Effect

In 1858, the *Charleston Mercury* declared:

> On the subject of slavery, the North and South...are not only two Peoples, but they are rival, hostile Peoples.

Review with students some of the causes for this division already covered in Part 1. Then refer them to the questions asked by the author on page 22. What new information do they expect to learn by digging deeper into the causes of the Civil War?

PART 2 | THE GROWING CRISIS

CHAPTERS 3–10
3 Harriet and *Uncle Tom* 23
4 Harriet, Also Known As Moses 27
5 Abraham Lincoln 34
6 New Salem 38
7 Mr. President Lincoln 41
8 President Jefferson Davis 45
9 Slavery 48
10 John Brown's Body 54

THE BIG IDEAS

Between 1830 and 1860, the conflict over slavery intensified as abolitionists and fugitive slaves exposed the evils of the South's "peculiar institution." As one proslavery South Carolinian lamented:

> We may shut our eyes and avert our faces, if we please, but there it is, the dark and growing evil at our doors....What is to be done? Oh! My God, I do not know, but something must be done.

By 1860, many white Southerners felt so embattled that they saw only one course of action open to them—secession. Part 2 explores the events that led them to this conclusion, and the two men who would lead in the war that followed.

INTRODUCING PART 2

SETTING GOALS

Introduce Part 2 by asking students if one individual really makes a difference in the world. Have students discuss examples of people who have changed the course of history, and how they did it. Explain that Part 2 focuses on Harriet Beecher Stowe, Harriet Tubman, Abraham Lincoln, and Jefferson Davis, four individuals who influenced the course of American history.)

To set goals for Part 2, tell students that they will
- describe the roles and importance of key figures: Stowe, Tubman, Lincoln, and Davis.
- debate the ethics of civil disobedience.
- chart the laws that controlled the institution of slavery.
- discuss the differing opinions of slavery after the Lincoln-Douglas debates of 1858.
- judge whether the actions of John Brown make him a martyr or a madman.

SETTING A CONTEXT FOR READING

Thinking About the Big Ideas   To open Part 2, help students focus and articulate their feelings about the lack of liberty endured by enslaved people. First ask them to read aloud the marginal accounts of slavery on pages 28, 29, 30, and 50. Then ask them to imagine that they lived in the North in the 1850s. How would such stories affect their opinion of slavery? How might their opinion affect the growing conflict between North and South? For example, how might each of the following respond to these stories: Abraham Lincoln, an abolitionist, a Southern slave owner, a supporter of John Calhoun?

Interpreting Primary Sources   Before students begin Part 2, read aloud the quote from Solomon Northup in the caption on page 29. Students should try to visualize what Northup and others lived through. You might also relate that Northup was born and raised a free man, but was kidnapped and enslaved for many years. After sharing what they imagined, have students examine the photograph on page 29. Ask students if they agree with the phrase "a picture is worth a thousand words."

SETTING A CONTEXT IN SPACE AND TIME

Using Maps   Refer students to the Slavery—Then and Now feature on pages 50-51. Using a wall map or an atlas, ask students to flag nations that had abolished slavery and/or serfdom by 1861. (Canada ended slavery in 1826.) The United States prided itself as the protector of liberty. How might other nations have challenged that claim in the 1850s? If war between the North and South came, how might the existence of slavery affect opinion in the international community? Students should save their answers to check against later chapters.

Establishing a Context in Time   Many students have difficulty studying disconnected events occurring in the same time. One way to link these events is to establish a context using the life of an individual. Tell students that Abraham Lincoln was born in 1809. Ask them to use their books or other resources to find out how old Lincoln was when each of the following events occurred: Thomas Jefferson leaves presidency (*1809—a month old*), Illinois becomes state (*1816—7 years*), Monroe Doctrine (*1823—14 years*), Jackson elected President (*1828—19 years*), Battle of the Alamo (*1836—27 years*), first telegraph message sent (*1844—35 years*) California Gold Rush (*1849—40 years*), *Uncle Tom's Cabin* published (*1852—43 years*), Civil War begins (*1861—52 years*). Have them guess how each event may have influenced Lincoln.

GEOGRAPHY CONNECTIONS

Have students locate Litchfield, Connecticut (in the northwestern part of the state), and Cincinnati, Ohio, on a map. Ask them to explain how Harriet Beecher Stowe's move from Connecticut to Ohio influenced her knowledge of and interest in the dispute over slavery. (*The move from New England—far from slavery—to Ohio—just across the river from slavery—gave her a close look at the world of slavery.*)

MEETING INDIVIDUAL NEEDS

Most students should be able to read *Uncle Tom's Cabin*. You may ask students to read the book or excerpts from the book, and then use the material to supplement your discussion in Part 2.

CHAPTER 3
HARRIET AND *UNCLE TOM*
PAGES 23-26

1 Class Period   **Homework: Student Study Guide p. 12**

Chapter Summary

A woman barely five feet tall used a pen to touch the hearts and minds of a nation. Harriet Beecher Stowe, gave slavery a human face and inspired many Northerners to embrace abolition.

Key Vocabulary
dialect   plantation   overseer

1. CONNECT

To help students understand the importance of *Uncle Tom's Cabin*, write *catalyst* on the chalkboard. Discuss that, just as one chemical can cause a reaction, one person or event or publication can spark momentous change. Ask students to describe any book, TV show, or movie that has had a profound effect on them or modern society.

2. UNDERSTAND

1. Read up to the second complete paragraph on page 25. Discuss: What experiences in Beecher's childhood do you think affected her opinions of slavery? (*attitudes of father, inquiry within family, personal observations of slavery*)
2. Read the rest of the chapter. Discuss: The author says Stowe "tried to be fair" when she wrote *Uncle Tom's Cabin*. What does she mean? (*She tried to show the evils of slavery independent of color or region.*) Why was *Uncle Tom's Cabin* unique? (*It portrayed enslaved Africans as people, made a black man the hero, and placed a human face on slavery.*)
3. Have students read the selection from *Uncle Tom's Cabin* on Resource Page 3 (TG page 101).

3. CHECK UNDERSTANDING

Writing   Have students write a short paragraph explaining why Harriet Beecher Stowe decided to write *Uncle Tom's Cabin* and how she must have felt when the book became so successful.

Thinking About the Chapter (Drawing Inferences)   Engage the class in a discussion of the meaning of Lincoln's remark to Stowe (see page 26). Have them give concrete details of how the book affected attitudes both North and South. (*Lead students to understand how empathy aroused by the book made many Northerners more willing to fight a war to end slavery. Southerners became more angry and threatened.*)

4 HARRIET, ALSO KNOWN AS MOSES
PAGES 27-33

1 Class Period   **Homework: Student Study Guide p. 13**

Chapter Summary
Another Harriet—Harriet Tubman—destroyed the argument that slavery was a positive good. By leading hundreds of slaves out of the South, she demonstrated the willingness of people in slavery to risk death in pursuit of liberty.

Key Vocabulary
Underground Railroad   stations   passengers
conductors   civil disobedience

1. CONNECT

Have students tell what they already know about Harriet Tubman. Then ask the class why Harriet Tubman was also known as Moses. *(Moses led the Israelites out of slavery in Egypt, and Tubman led Africans out of slavery in the South.)*

2. UNDERSTAND

1. Read pages 27-30. Discuss: What experiences in Harriet Tubman's childhood helped shape her into a fierce opponent of slavery? *(brutal treatment while a slave; seeing other slaves, including her sisters, sold away from their families)*
2. Read the rest of the chapter. Discuss the terminology of the Underground Railroad. *(station, conductor, passenger, etc.)* What specific obstacles and hardships did Harriet Tubman and her passengers have to endure? *(slave catchers, bad weather, crying babies, lack of food and water, only the North Star as a guide, etc.)*

3. CHECK UNDERSTANDING

Writing   Have students write a one-page diary entry as if they are traveling on the Underground Railroad. Set the scene for them: traveling at night with a baby and small children, freezing rain, unknown woods with no map, sick or elderly people in the party, barking dogs not far behind.

Thinking About the Chapter (Evaluating)   Tell students that Congress is about to approve money for a monument to the most important female abolitionist. Harriet Beecher Stowe and Harriet Tubman are the two finalists, but the government has money for only one monument. Have students use the details from Chapters 3 and 4 to decide what should be done.

GEOGRAPHY CONNECTIONS
Have students use a detailed wall map to trace the following Underground Railroad route: Depart from Memphis. Travel to safe houses in Cairo, Illinois; Terre Haute, Indiana; and Kalamazoo, Michigan. Final stop—and safety—is Windsor, Canada. Ask them to calculate the miles between each stop and the cumulative mileage.

ACTIVITIES/JOHNS HOPKINS TEAM LEARNING
See the Student Team Learning Activity on TG page 46.

HISTORY ARCHIVES
A History of US Sourcebook
1. #35, From William Lloyd Garrison, *The Liberator*, vol. 1, no. 1 (1831)
2. #36, From *A North Carolina Law Forbidding the Teaching of Slaves to Read and Write* (1831)

LINKING DISCIPLINES
History/Art
On page 28 is a beautiful painting of passengers on the Underground Railroad. Ask students how the artist has romanticized the scene. *(traveling by day, light—freedom—in the distance, women wearing jewelry and everyone looking fresh, and so on)* Then discuss why the artist might have painted this romantic view instead of a more realistic one.

MEETING INDIVIDUAL NEEDS
Visual learners may benefit by seeing copies of the series of paintings Jacob Lawrence created depicting the life of Harriet Tubman.

NOTE FROM THE AUTHOR
Hardly anyone escapes the judgment of history. Did Harriet Tubman have any idea that schoolchildren would be reading about her more than 100 years after she lived? Not likely. But what she did was courageous and right anyway, and it has made it into everyone's history book. What does that teach kids? A whole lot.

READING NONFICTION

CHAPTER 5

READING NONFICTION

Analyzing Text Organization

Have students identify the text organization of this chapter. (*chronological*) Ask students why the author chose this structure rather than cause and effect or compare and contrast. (*The author is telling the story of Lincoln's early life, which lends itself to a chronological structure.*)

ABRAHAM LINCOLN

PAGES 34–37

1 Class Period   **Homework: Student Study Guide p. 14**

Chapter Summary

Many elements went into shaping the life and thought of Abraham Lincoln, including the strength born of frontier living and the values of a family opposed to human bondage.

Key Vocabulary

blab school

1. CONNECT

Chapters 5-7 detail the life of Abraham Lincoln. Chapter 5 emphasizes Lincoln's frontier roots. Before reading the chapter define *frontier* with students and ask what type of people tend to be successful on the frontier. (*hard working, self-reliant, tough*)

2. UNDERSTAND

1. Read pages 34-36 up to "A man on the frontier...." Discuss: What were some of the challenges Lincoln's family faced on the frontier? (*Indian attack, primitive living conditions, death of a parent, wild animals, poor schools*) What experiences in Lincoln's childhood helped mold his attitude toward slavery? (*the religious and antislavery beliefs of his family; his family's move to the free state of Indiana*)
2. Read the rest of the chapter. Ask: What character traits became apparent early in Lincoln that probably helped him become one of the nation's greatest Presidents? (*Possible responses: love of learning, honesty, sense of humor, skill at oratory, personal strength, religious faith*)

3. CHECK UNDERSTANDING

Writing   Have students write a paragraph listing three reasons why it is important to study the early life of our Presidents, citing details from Chapter 5.

Thinking About the Chapter (Evaluating)   Engage the class in a discussion about whether Lincoln's childhood could be considered a "good" childhood. Ask: In what ways is Lincoln's childhood one that you would have wanted to live? (*Students might determine that, although Lincoln's life was very difficult by our standards, it was similar to many of the time. Moreover, maybe greatness comes from overcoming such challenges.*)

CHAPTER 6 NEW SALEM

PAGES 38-40

1 Class Period   Homework: Student Study Guide p. 14

Chapter Summary

Lincoln's love of book-learning led him away from the frontier to a series of jobs in Illinois. Here Lincoln jumped into politics and delivered his first speeches on the injustices of slavery.

Key Vocabulary

mentor   injustice
policy   hooligan

1. CONNECT

Just as Harriet Beecher Stowe's move to Ohio gave her new understanding of slavery, Lincoln's early life in Kentucky, Indiana, and Illinois gave him an understanding of ordinary people of the South and the North. Ask students who have moved how the experience has helped to expand their horizons.

2. UNDERSTAND

1. Read pages 38-39 up to "After the store failed...." Discuss: The author says New Salem was Lincoln's college. What experiences did Lincoln have in New Salem that prepared him for the future? *(shopkeeper, postmaster, scholar, surveyor, law student, political candidate)* Was he an immediate success? *(No, he failed in business and had to pay off a large debt.)*
2. Read the rest of the chapter. Discuss: What training enabled Lincoln to become a successful lawyer and member of the Illinois General Assembly? *(became well known as postmaster, read and studied law)* What did Lincoln's early experience in the state legislature reveal about his political style? *(Possible response: He spoke his mind when it mattered, and he followed his conscience.)*

3. CHECK UNDERSTANDING

Writing   Ask students to imagine that Lincoln were alive today. Have them write a paragraph from his point of view discussing the merits of today's schools and the role of lifelong education.

Thinking About the Chapter (Comparing and Contrasting)
Have students imagine they live in New Salem in 1831 when Lincoln arrived. (You might explain that he was in his early twenties, and described himself as a "piece of floating driftwood.") Ask them to compare and contrast Lincoln on his arrival and on his departure for Springfield in 1837. How had he changed and how had he stayed the same?

READING NONFICTION
Analyzing Point of View

Ask partners to list evidence the author gives to support her point of view that New Salem was Lincoln's college. Have them categorize the evidence into facts, anecdotes, opinions, and primary source quotations. Discuss how the information the author includes shows that Lincoln was an educated man despite his lack of formal education.

MORE ABOUT...
Lincoln's Political Career

In 1846, Lincoln was elected to the House of Representatives. His outspoken denunciation of President Polk and the Mexican War destroyed his chances of reelection in 1848. Lincoln feared his days in politics were over.

Lincoln and Education

When asked about the study of law, Lincoln once said, "Get the books, and read and study them till you understand them....The books, and your capacity to understand them, are just the same in all places....Always bear in mind that your own resolution to succeed, is more important than any other one thing."

CHAPTER 7

MR. PRESIDENT LINCOLN

PAGES 41–44

Have students complete Resource Page 4 (TG page 102) to illustrate how torn the nation was in 1860 when Lincoln was elected President. Mention to students that Lincoln's name was not even allowed on the ballot of many Southern states.

HISTORY ARCHIVES

A History of US Sourcebook

1. #49, From Abraham Lincoln, *"A House Divided": Address to the Illinois Republican Convention* (1858)

2. #50, From Abraham Lincoln, *Debate with Stephen Douglas* (1858)

MORE ABOUT...

Election of Senators

U.S. Senators were elected by state legislatures well into the 20th century. In 1858, more Illinois voters cast their ballots for candidates for the state legislature who supported Lincoln than for those who supported Douglas. But because of inequitable districting, more Douglas supporters were elected, and Douglas was chosen to be Senator.

LINKING DISCIPLINES

History/Art

Have partners or small groups prepare an 1860 presidential campaign poster for Lincoln. The poster should celebrate Lincoln's frontier upbringing and the character traits that make him the best choice for President.

1 Class Period   ·   Homework: Student Study Guide p. 15

Chapter Summary

Abraham Lincoln tried to avoid hatred by attacking slavery rather than the people who practiced it. His forceful defense of liberty for enslaved Africans during the Lincoln-Douglas debates helped thrust Lincoln into the White House—and the South out of the Union.

Key Vocabulary

popular sovereignty   despotism
fugitive slave law   abolitionist

1. CONNECT

This chapter focuses on the 1858 U.S. Senate campaign between Lincoln and Douglas. The issue splitting the nation was whether to allow slavery in the territories acquired from Mexico. Explain that the Lincoln-Douglas debates were another part of the argument over slavery that dated back to the Constitutional Convention.

2. UNDERSTAND

1. Read pages 41-42. Discuss: Contrast the opinions of Lincoln and Douglas on slavery. (*Lincoln thought slavery was wrong, and was against its spread to the territories. Douglas believed that the voters in the territories should decide the slavery issue for themselves.*)

2. Read the rest of the chapter. Ask: Was Lincoln an abolitionist? Why? (*Possible responses: He was not, because he advocated stopping the spread of slavery, not destroying it. He was, because he wanted slavery to end.*) How did the debates hand Lincoln the keys to the White House? (*They won Lincoln national attention and a chance to make his political views known.*)

3. CHECK UNDERSTANDING

Writing   Have students write a dialogue between Lincoln and Douglas in which the two men debate slavery.

Thinking About the Chapter (Analyzing)   Have the class explore the meaning of Lincoln's "House Divided" speech on pages 43-44. Discuss whether Lincoln was right to suggest that the country could not stand if it were divided over slavery. Ask students if there are any issues today that are so potentially divisive.

CHAPTER 8 | PRESIDENT JEFFERSON DAVIS
PAGES 45–47

1 Class Period   Homework: Student Study Guide p. 16

Chapter Summary

Jefferson Davis's path led him from the frontier into the Deep South, where his family became prosperous plantation owners. Here he followed in the footsteps of John Calhoun, becoming the region's most skilled defender of states' rights.

Key Vocabulary

intolerant   secede

1. CONNECT

When Jefferson Davis was born in 1808, he was named after the current president, Thomas Jefferson. Davis, like Jefferson, believed that states had the right to nullify an unjust federal law. Each man also owned slaves. Yet some people describe Davis as a traitor and hail Jefferson as a Founding Father. Is this fair?

2. UNDERSTAND

1. Read the chapter. Discuss: What experiences in Davis's childhood helped mold his attitude toward slavery? (*He grew up on his brother's plantation and benefited from life supported by slavery.*) The author notes that Davis was a "model slave owner." What does that mean? (*Lead students to understand that although Jefferson treated his slaves more fairly than did some other slave owners, slavery by definition is cruel because it denies liberty.*)
2. What skills did Davis bring to the Confederate presidency? (*great intellect, military experience, experience in the U.S. Senate*)

3. CHECK UNDERSTANDING

Writing   Have students write a short essay comparing the lives of Jefferson Davis and Abraham Lincoln. They should discuss three similarities and three differences.

Thinking About the Chapter (Drawing Conclusions)   On page 47 the author quotes Zachary Taylor. Engage the class in a discussion of Taylor's quote that some Southern politicians were "intolerant and revolutionary." In what ways was Jefferson Davis intolerant and revolutionary? (*Davis and others like Calhoun had trouble seeing the other side of the states' rights or slavery debate. By 1860, there was no middle ground and the only option for many was to secede from the Union.*)

READING NONFICTION

Analyzing Sequence

Have students create a time line of Jefferson Davis's life beginning with his birth and ending with his becoming president of the Confederacy. Students should place 7-10 events in order on the time line.

READING NONFICTION

Analyzing Graphic Aids

Ask students to study all the illustrations in the chapter. Then ask them to decide which ones could have been used as propaganda for the continuation of slavery (*illustrations of Nat Turner and L'Ouverture*) and against slavery (*the rest of the illustrations*).

MEETING INDIVIDUAL NEEDS

Visual learners and others will enjoy Gordon Parks's film adaptation of Solomon Northup's autobiography. The film, *Half-Slave, Half-Free*, details the life of Northup, who was born free in New York. He was kidnapped and spent 12 years in bondage before being rescued. The film puts a human face on slavery. It shows how people tried to maintain their dignity under a brutal system, and how men and women, black and white, were forced to make compromising decisions to survive.

CHAPTER 9 | SLAVERY

PAGES 48–53

1-2 Class Periods   Homework: Student Study Guide p. 17

Chapter Summary

The Founders expected slavery to wither in a land of liberty, and it did in the North. However, in the South, slavery became even more prosperous and institutionalized. As other nations began to end slavery, the American South found itself more isolated.

Key Vocabulary

slave trade   fugitive

1. CONNECT

Have students list reasons that people living in a nation founded on liberty might give for keeping a certain group of people in bondage. Have students evaluate the morality of such reasons.

2. UNDERSTAND

1. Read the main text of the chapter. Discuss: Why did an illegal slave trade continue after 1808? (*It was very profitable; some Southerners supported it.*) How did the revolts of Nat Turner and Toussaint L'Ouverture change slavery in the South? (*Their revolts created great fear amongst Southern plantation owners. Southern legislatures passed harsh laws that made life even more difficult for the slaves.*)
2. Ask: What does the author say the South really needed? (*new ways of thinking; change in its economy*) What did it do instead? (*blamed the North for its troubles, followed old practices*)
3. Read the Slavery—Then and Now feature (pages 50-51). Discuss: How were ideas about slavery changing elsewhere in the world? (*Haiti, Canada, and many European nations had banned the practice.*)

3. CHECK UNDERSTANDING

Writing   Write an essay describing ways that Southerners used laws and argument to protect the institution of slavery.

Thinking About the Chapter (Synthesizing)   Moderate a class debate on the proposition that the Fugitive Slave Law forcing the return of Anthony Burns is unconstitutional. Students must make reference to the Constitution (not including the post-Civil War amendments) to support their arguments, including the sections pertaining to property and the rights of citizens. You may wish to play devil's advocate to ensure that both sides of the argument are presented. Use any strong emotions that result to illustrate the emotions felt by people before the Civil War.

10 JOHN BROWN'S BODY

PAGES 54-58

1 Class Period   Homework: Student Study Guide p. 18

Chapter Summary

Today people still debate which label best applies to John Brown—hero martyr or crazed fanatic. In 1859, the debate solidified the division between North and South.

Key Vocabulary

strategic   guerrilla war   treason   martyr

1. CONNECT

Have students recall the Boston Tea Party. Remind them that the Americans who raided the British ships are seen as heroes in American history. Explain that John Brown's raid on Harpers Ferry was one of the sparks that ignited the Civil War, but that Brown's legacy is much more controversial.

2. UNDERSTAND

1. Read the chapter. Discuss: What motivated John Brown's actions in the 1850s? (*He wanted to end slavery.*) What did Brown hope to accomplish by his raid on Harpers Ferry? (*He hoped to spark a large-scale slave uprising that would sweep through the South.*) What was Brown willing to risk for his cause? (*death of himself, his followers, and slaveowners*)
2. What question did Brown raise at his trial and in his last note to his executioner? (*whether slavery could be ended with anything but bloodshed*) Why did Lincoln disagree with Brown's action? (*because Brown resorted to violence, bloodshed, and an attack on a federal arsenal*)

3. CHECK UNDERSTANDING

Writing   Have students study the excerpt from the poem by Oliver Wendell Holmes on page 57. Ask them to write a short essay about the excerpt. One paragraph should explain the meaning of Holmes's lines (the influence of *Uncle Tom's Cabin* and John Brown on the Civil War); another paragraph should discuss who the students think "was mightier of the two."

Thinking About the Chapter (Making Judgments)   When you have finished the chapter, ask the class whether John Brown should be seen as a hero martyr or a madman. (*Responses will vary, but ask students to think hard about whether the use of violence is ever justified to change society.*) Extend the discussion by asking whether John Brown was successful in achieving his goals. (*Although Brown failed at Harpers Ferry, his actions polarized a nation and helped spark the civil war that ended slavery.*)

GEOGRAPHY CONNECTIONS

Civil War Room Activity

Have students continue the Civil War Room activity as described on TG page 26. Have them locate and mark the following:

Harpers Ferry   39°15'N 77°40'W

Ask them to examine the map on page 55. Have them analyze why John Brown might have picked Harpers Ferry as the place to attempt his rebellion. (*intersection of two important rivers and a railroad junction; mountains nearby to help guerrilla fighting; relatively close to the North for support or escape*)

HISTORY ARCHIVES

A History of US Sourcebook

#51, John Brown, *Last Statement to the Court* (1859)

MEETING INDIVIDUAL NEEDS

Students can perform a choral rendition of the song "John Brown's Body" on page 152. If anyone in the class plays an instrument, have them play the music while the others sing.

MORE ABOUT...

Brown and Douglass

Brown had a secret meeting with Frederick Douglass and invited him to join the raid. Brown felt that Douglass' leadership ability and stature would make him an ideal leader in the slave revolt. Douglass declined. Although he respected Brown's zeal for the antislavery cause, he could not support Brown's use of violence to end slavery.

JOHNS HOPKINS TEAM LEARNING

TWO HARRIETS

1 EXTENDED CLASS PERIOD

FOCUS ACTIVITY

1. Organize the class into teams of four students each to answer the question, "What is a heroine?"

2. Have teams use Roundtable to brainstorm the characteristics of a heroine.

STUDENT TEAM LEARNING ACTIVITY/LOCATING AND RECORDING INFORMATION

1. Have teams divide up into two partnerships, with each partnership choosing one of the two Harriets to research. (See Chapters 3 and 4.) Each partnership should create a graphic organizer, such as a web, to record information about the woman's major achievements, her early life, and important events in her life. Partnerships should use the information to make a Wanted Poster about the woman. The details should be included to emphasize why the woman is wanted. (*Wanted* can be construed in a positive or negative way.)

2. Each partnership should share their information with the rest of the team. Teams should discuss the contributions each woman made to ending slavery.

3. Circulate and Monitor As the teams work, systematically visit them. If necessary, help students read, locate, and record appropriate information about Stowe and Tubman. Answer any questions and help students complete the task in a timely, accurate, and complete manner.

4. Use Numbered Heads to have teams share information and discuss the heroic characteristics of the two Harriets. Ask students to compare these characteristics to the ones they brainstormed in the focus activity.

Part 2 Check-Up   Use Check-Up 2 (TG page 94) to assess student learning in Part 2.

ALTERNATE ASSESSMENT

Ask students to write an essay answering one of the following questions, which link the big ideas across chapters.

1. Making Connections   In what ways were *Uncle Tom's Cabin* and the Underground Railroad linked to the growing conflict over slavery? (*Both the book and stories told by fugitives made Northerners more willing to fight to end slavery.*)

2. Making Connections   Why did America fight a Civil War in 1861? Explain the underlying causes of the war and the immediate events that sparked the explosion. (*Students should first look at the root causes of slavery and states' rights and then discuss several specific events including John Brown, Lincoln's election, rise of abolitionism, etc.*)

DEBATING THE ISSUES

Use the topics below to stimulate debate:

1. Resolved   That Harriet Beecher Stowe (or Harriet Tubman or John Brown or Nat Turner) had the best strategy for ending slavery. (Organize this as a panel discussion, with volunteers role-playing—and researching—the personalities named.)

2. Resolved   That John Brown should be pardoned for his attack on Harper's Ferry. (Appoint students to represent the various opinions mentioned in the text and in marginal notes. To stimulate interest, you might hold a mock trial of Brown, and then have the debate take place among members of the jury. The rest of the class should take notes on the major points scored for each side, and then arrive at a class verdict.)

MAKING ETHICAL JUDGMENTS

The following activities ask students to consider issues of ethics. Be sure that students can define *ethics* (a system of beliefs about right and wrong) as used in the title of the feature on pages 32-33 in Book Six.

1. On pages 32-33, the author asks some tough questions: What do you do if you think a law is evil? Do you break it? Answer these questions from the perspectives of John Brown and Martin Luther King, Jr. Working with several other classmates, create a dialogue in which Brown and King discuss their approaches to unjust laws. (Differences will rest in Brown's willingness to resort to violence. King rejected laws but respected the legal process, including willingness to be jailed as the penalty for civil disobedience.)

NOTE FROM THE AUTHOR

People were always telling funny stories about President Lincoln, but he told the best ones about himself. There was the time two Quaker women were arguing about who was the better president: Abraham Lincoln or Jefferson Davis. "I think Jefferson Davis will triumph," said one of them. "Why does thee think so?" said the other. "Because Jefferson is a praying man," said the first. "Abraham is a praying man too," said the second. To which the first replied, "Yes, but the Lord will think Abraham is joking."

When a foreign diplomat stopped at the White House he came upon the President polishing his shoes. "Mr. President," he said in great surprise, "do you black your own boots?" "Yes," said Lincoln, "whose do you black?"

Ask your students how they feel about someone who does a lot of joking. Is it dignified? Is it right for a President? What about someone who is able to laugh at himself? What does that say about him?

USING THE RUBRICS

To assess these writing assignments, group projects, and activities, scoring rubrics have been provided at the back of this Teaching Guide. Be sure to explain the rubrics to your students.

2. After reading the primary source passages from Resource Page 11 (TG page 109), have students discuss the issue of provocation in the Nat Turner Rebellion. Both accounts of the rebellion state that Nat Turner had no specific, immediate grievance against his owner. But what were the larger grievances? Have students discuss the larger provocations and grievances that Nat Turner and his followers had. Have the students discuss whether Nat Turner's methods, and the murders of 70 men, women and children were justified. Does forced slavery justify the murders of the slaveholders? Why or why not? You may wish to compare Nat Turner's motives with John Brown's, or with current controversial figures from world events.

PROJECTS AND ACTIVITIES

Writing Theater Reviews   Have students imagine they are theater critics watching the opening of the stage version of *Uncle Tom's Cabin.* Divide the class into groups and appoint some to act as reporters from major Southern cities such as Charleston or Savannah. Have others represent newspapers in Northern cities such as Boston or New York. Direct still others to write for a London newspaper. Have each group—using reviews from a local newspaper as models—write critiques of the play. What does each review reveal about the impact of Stowe's novel?

Delivering a Monologue   Review the closeness of Abraham Lincoln to his sister Sarah and that of Jefferson Davis to his brother Joseph. Request volunteers to deliver monologues in which Sarah and Joseph recall the early years of their famous siblings.

Comparing Points of View   Hand out copies of the following quote by Stephen Douglas:

> *Let each State mind its own business and...there will be no trouble....If we stand by that principle, then Mr. Lincoln will find that this Republic can exist forever divided into free and slave States as our fathers [the Founders] made it.*

Have students compare this quote with the statement made by Lincoln on page 43. How do the two views differ? Suppose Douglas had won the presidency. Would the Union eventually have split anyway? Why or why not?

Using Historical Imagination   Ask students to imagine that Jefferson Davis ran for President in 1860 against Abraham Lincoln. Request two volunteers to research and take the parts of the candidates. Then conduct a press conference in which the other students ask the candidates questions about their policies concerning the issues of the day—Fugitive Slave Law, states' rights, abolition, and so on. You might allow each candidate to select one or two campaign advisers to help answer questions.

Developing an Argument   Read aloud the remark by Albert Gallatin Brown on page 51 that slavery was "a blessing for the slave, and a blessing for the master." Have students work in small groups to assemble information that an abolitionist might have used to disprove this statement. You may wish to distribute Resource Page 12 (TG page 110), which contains a passage from Theodore Weld, an abolitionist leader. Encourage students to use quotes from enslaved Africans or photos in their book, as well as further readings and research. Have students present their arguments in the form of speeches delivered at an abolitionist rally, using Weld's speech as a model.

Turning Pictures into Words   Have students refer to the pictures in the poster on page 53 and prepare a written account of Burns's story. Encourage them to read the details in each picture to determine the artist's point of view. That is, how does the artist want people to view the incident? Direct students to slant their writing in the same way that the artist slants the art.

LOOKING AHEAD

Making Predictions

On April 29, 1861, Jefferson Davis made the following announcement to the Confederate Congress:

> *Gentlemen of the Congress:—It is my pleasing duty to announce to you that the Constitution framed for the establishment of a permanent government of the Confederate States of America has been ratified by the several conventions of each of those States which were referred to to inaugurate the said government...upon...[the] basis of popular will.*

Ask students to restate this message in their own words. What dilemmas did it pose for Abraham Lincoln, President of the United States of America? What did the use of the terms Confederate and United imply about the two governments?

CHAPTERS 11-14

11 Lincoln's Problems 59
12 The Union Generals 64
13 The Confederate Generals 68
14 President Davis's Problems 73

THE BIG IDEAS

In an 1862 letter to Horace Greeley, President Lincoln clearly stated his war goals:

My paramount object in this struggle is to save the Union, and is not either to save or destroy Slavery. If I could save the Union without freeing any slave, I would do it; and if I could do it by freeing some and leaving others alone, I would also do that....I have here stated my purpose according to my view of official duty, and I intend no modification of my oft-expressed personal wish that all men, everywhere, could be free.

Supporters of abolition criticized Lincoln for not moving more forcefully on the issue of slavery. But Lincoln did not want to risk losing slave-holding border states. Lincoln also faced enormous problems early in the war as he searched for capable military leadership. Jefferson Davis had excellent generals throughout the war, but faced the daunting issues of few resources, lack of allies, and uninspiring political leadership.

INTRODUCING PART 3

SETTING GOALS

Introduce Part 3 by asking students if they agree with the old saying, "All is fair in love and war." Then discuss how Lincoln imprisoned many members of the Maryland state legislature just before they voted on secession. *(The remaining pro-Union representatives voted to keep the state in the Union.)* Students should understand the extraordinary conditions the war forced on leaders both North and South. To save democracy, leaders like Lincoln sometimes had to act undemocratically. If Maryland had sided with the Confederacy, Washington, D.C., would have been surrounded by secessionist states.

To set goals for Part 3, tell students that they will
- explain the progression of Southern secession and how Lincoln courted the border states of Maryland, Kentucky, Missouri, and Delaware.
- compare the advantages and disadvantages of the North and the South.
- list generals who served for the North and the South and explain the South's advantage in military leadership.

SETTING A CONTEXT FOR READING
Thinking About the Big Ideas   Students will have little trouble linking the idea of conflict with war. But they may be thinking in terms of bullets rather than feelings. Challenge students to put themselves in the shoes of the son or daughter of a Union or Confederate officer. What feelings might they have? Which of these feelings *conflict* with each other? (For example, the child might feel pride and fear.) Lead into a discussion of the personal

conflict faced by key characters. Read aloud the excerpt from Abraham Lincoln's letter to Horace Greeley above. Ask students to identify the conflict faced by Lincoln.

Comparing and Contrasting One of the most important activities for students to do before studying the fighting is to examine the relative strengths and weaknesses of the opponents. Distribute and discuss the Northern and Southern States economy maps found at the back of this guide. Have students complete Resource Page 5 (TG page 102), showing the economic differences between North and South at the beginning of the war. Have students hypothesize what advantages the South might have to offset Northern economic and manpower strengths. *(leadership, willingness to fight, need to fight defensive war only)*

SETTING A CONTEXT IN SPACE AND TIME

Using Maps You might have students speculate on the course of the war by referring them to the map on page 67. Ask students to speculate about which side would take the offensive. *(North)* How could they tell? *(by the direction of the arrows)* What seem to have been the North's military goals? *(to blockade the South's ports, to break the Confederacy in half by controlling the Mississippi River, to attack toward Richmond, Virginia, and other interior areas)* How might these aims change if the Border States joined the Confederacy? *(Responses should underscore the increased difficulty of success.)* Have students save their answers for comparison in Chapter 11.

Creating a Time Line The Civil War is a complex mass of events. To keep the war straight it is imperative for students to have some chronological structure. On page 153 there is a chronology of events for the war. Encourage students to refer to this list as often as they need to. Also, have them create a year-by-year illustrated time line that captures important information between 1861-1865. As students read and discuss, have them go back to their time lines and creatively represent an event, person, or act. By breaking the war up into manageable yearly chunks, students have a better chance of linking all the events together.

READING NONFICTION

Analyzing Rhetorical Devices

Discuss that the author often asks readers to think about "what if" questions such as those she poses at the end of page 60. Explain that the questions are part of Joy Hakim's rhetorical style and that she asks them to get readers to consider, as historians do, events that might have changed history. Have students use the map on page 67 to discuss if the capital could have been saved without Maryland.

GEOGRAPHY CONNECTIONS

Civil War Room Activity

Have students continue the Civil War Room activity as described on TG page 26. Using the map on page 67 of the Student Edition, have them outline and label the border states and discuss their strategic importance. (*Responses should include Maryland surrounding Washington, D.C. and the Chesapeake Bay; Kentucky controlling the Ohio River; Missouri bordering Illinois and controlling the Mississippi River; and Delaware controlling access to the Delaware River and Philadelphia.*)

ACTIVITIES/JOHNS HOPKINS TEAM LEARNING

See the Student Team Learning Activity on TG page 56.

MORE ABOUT...

Brethren in Arms

Only 15 years earlier, at West Point, the Confederate commander at Charleston, General Pierre Gustave Toutant Beauregard, had been a student of the Union commander of Fort Sumter, Major William Anderson.

CHAPTER 11 LINCOLN'S PROBLEMS

PAGES 59–63

1 Class Period   Homework: Student Study Guide p. 19

Chapter Summary

Lincoln knew he had to wage an offensive war, but he dared not lose the support of citizens or wary border states. Knowing that many Northerners were still unready to fight a war against slavery, he refused to drag abolition onto the battlefield.

Key Vocabulary

per capita	industrial hub	border states
secede	shinplaster	

1. CONNECT

Have the class imagine Lincoln's feelings as the Southern states left the Union, each one claiming that Lincoln's election threatened their way of life. Was this fair, or had extremists taken over the South?

2. UNDERSTAND

1. Read through the first complete paragraph on page 61. Discuss: What were the reasons for each wave of Southern secessions? (*The first wave seceded over states' rights and slavery—see Chapter 10. The second wave seceded because they would not fight their sister states.*) What problems did the border states present Lincoln? (*If he freed the slaves, the border states would probably secede.*)
2. Read the rest of the chapter. Ask: Why didn't Lincoln move quickly on slavery? (*Northerners weren't fully behind a war to end slavery. He had to consider the border states.*) What started the war? (*Confederates opened fire on Fort Sumter.*)

3. CHECK UNDERSTANDING

Writing   Have students imagine they are Southern newspaper editors and write editorials on Lincoln's attempts to hold the border states and the bombardment of Fort Sumter.

Thinking About the Chapter (Analyzing)   Have students consider Lincoln's strategy concerning Fort Sumter. His decision to hold the fort and resupply it led to the Confederates firing on the fort. Ask: What did Lincoln achieve by following this strategy rather than some more active strategy? Have students consider Lincoln's speeches up to that point.

CHAPTER 12

THE UNION GENERALS

PAGES 64–67

1 Class Period   Homework: Student Study Guide p. 20

Chapter Summary

General Winfield Scott handed Lincoln the plan to defeat the Confederacy. But Lincoln lacked the officers to carry it out until a rumpled, unorthodox general named Ulysses S. Grant came to his attention by winning victories in the West.

Key Vocabulary

blockade   Anaconda Plan   blockade runners

1. CONNECT

Write *leader* on the chalkboard. Have students brainstorm a list of qualities that make a good leader and give examples of leaders they know. Ask if a good leader needs to have most of these traits, or just some of them. Elicit the qualities a general must have during war. *(intelligence, decisiveness, flexibility, air of command, inspirational)*

2. UNDERSTAND

1. Read pages 64-65. Discuss: Describe General Scott's war plan and how it was received by others in the North. *(Known as the Anaconda Plan, it envisioned splitting the South in two along the Mississippi and squeezing it by attacks from the North and a blockade of its ports. Northerners laughed at it because it would take so long.)*
2. Read the rest of the chapter. Draw a comparison chart on the chalkboard for McClellan and Grant. Have students list the characteristics of both generals.

3. CHECK UNDERSTANDING

Writing   Have students write a short paragraph explaining why Ulysses S. Grant was just the sort of general to lead the type of war that President Lincoln needed to fight.

Thinking About the Chapter (Interpreting Pictures)   Have students examine the pictures of McClellan and Grant on pages 65-66. Then ask volunteers to role play a conversation between the men on how best to fight and win the war. Students should use the pictures and the text to help create a demeanor and even a style of language that might have been used by each man.

READING NONFICTION

Analyzing Word Choice

Have students come up with another appropriate name for Scott's war plan that captures the expected result of the plan.

GEOGRAPHY CONNECTIONS

Using the blank Eastern US Relief reproducible map, have students sketch the Anaconda Plan, labeling Scott's major strategic aims. Have students keep this map in their history journals, to compare with the North's actual tactics. Make sure students realize that although Scott's plan was roundly criticized initially, the North's overall strategy turned out to be much like the one he proposed. Ask why the South did not develop a similar strategy. (*They needed only to fight a defensive war.*) What might the South's war plan be called? (*Responses will vary.*)

Analyzing Word Choice

Ask partners to make a list of adjectives the author uses to describe the generals of the North (Chapter 12) and of the South (Chapter 13). Then discuss what these two lists tell them about the author's view on the abilities of the Union and Confederate high commands. (*Except for Grant and Sherman, the Union generals were vastly inferior to the Confederate command.*)

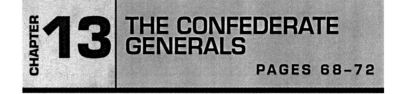

CHAPTER 13 THE CONFEDERATE GENERALS

PAGES 68-72

1 Class Period   **Homework: Student Study Guide p. 21**

Chapter Summary

A tradition of soldiering gave the Confederacy some of the war's most talented generals. One of the most able and respected was Robert E. Lee—a heroic figure to many Americans, who faced a very difficult decision even before the war began.

Key Vocabulary

patriarch   invincibility

1. CONNECT

To help students understand Lee's decision to fight for the South, discuss the meaning of patriotism. Elicit that it means loyalty and pride in one's country, but that in the early decades of the United States Americans felt patriotism for their own state. Ask students for what they feel loyalty and pride, and if their feelings might conflict.

2. UNDERSTAND

1. Read page 68. Discuss: Why did the South have so many good military officers? (*It had a long tradition of soldiering in which some of the best and brightest young men became officers.*)
2. Read the rest of the chapter. Ask: Why did both Jackson and Lee inspire such devotion from the soldiers who fought with them? (*Both men were military geniuses who demanded a lot of their soldiers and themselves.*) What might have happened if Lee had accepted Lincoln's offer? (*The war might have been much shorter.*)

3. CHECK UNDERSTANDING

Writing   Have students reread The Great Stonewall on page 71. Ask them to imagine that they are fighting a war in which their homeland was being invaded. Have them write a paragraph explaining whether they would want to be a soldier in an army led by Stonewall Jackson.

Thinking About the Chapter (Speculating)   Raise the question of loyalty to one's state conflicting with loyalty to one's country, and what a difficult decision Lee had to make at the start of the Civil War. You may wish to have one team of students stand up to represent "Virginia" Lee and one represent "U.S." Lee, and let them argue the points on either side. The class should finish by discussing why Lee was so certain about his final decision.

CHAPTER 14 PRESIDENT DAVIS'S PROBLEMS

PAGES 73-75

1 Class Period   Homework: Student Study Guide p. 22

Chapter Summary

President Davis had superb generals, but he lacked the manufacturing base to give them adequate supplies. He also lacked the personality and political power to mold a loose confederation into a centralized war machine. Such shortcomings would prove the South's undoing.

Key Vocabulary

feudal   Articles of Confederation

1. CONNECT

Have students recall the weaknesses of the Articles of Confederation. *(weak central government, inability to raise a national army, inability to tax effectively)* You might personalize the discussion by asking if families or classes function well when all the members do not work together.

2. UNDERSTAND

1. Read page 73. Discuss: What problems in the South offset the advantage of superb generals? *(lack of manufactured goods, shortage of supplies, poor transportation, lack of a strong central government to coordinate the war)*
2. Chart: Have students complete Resource Page 5 (TG page 103) to compare the Northern and Southern economies.
3. Read the rest of the chapter. Ask: Why did the South think England would help them win the war? Why did England hesitate? (*England relied on Southern cotton, but also had ethical conflicts over slavery.*) What advantages did a republican government give to the Union? *(a strong central government able to raise an army and taxes to support the war)*

3. CHECK UNDERSTANDING

Writing   Have students write a short essay identifying at least four problems facing the Confederacy. They should rank the problems in order of importance and explain their ranking.

Thinking About the Chapter (Hypothesizing)   England's decision not to side with the Confederacy proved fatal to the South. Have students hypothesize what might have happened if the many pro-Confederate leaders in England had gotten their way. Remind students that England had the world's most powerful army and navy.

MEETING INDIVIDUAL NEEDS

There are many names used for the two sides in the Civil War. You may wish to have students list the names for the North and the South, as well as for Northerners and Southerners, in their notebooks as they come across them.

JOHNS HOPKINS TEAM LEARNING

THE WOMEN'S WAR

JOHNS HOPKINS
U N I V E R S I T Y

1 EXTENDED CLASS PERIOD

FOCUS ACTIVITY

1. Have volunteers define "home front" and describe the people and the situation there. Elicit details about home fronts that students have read about in *A History of US.* *(Revolutionary War)*

2. Ask students to tell about any home front situations they know about from family or friends. For instance, their grandparents may have told them stories dating to World War II or the Korean War, and their parents may have experienced it during the Vietnam War or later conflicts. Have them determine how the home front differs between limited wars such as the Gulf War of 1991 and major wars such as World War II. *(In limited wars, the home front is often restricted to the families of the soldiers. In major wars, the home front is the entire country.)*

STUDENT TEAM LEARNING ACTIVITY/ANALYZING A PRIMARY SOURCE

1. Divide the class into teams of four. Make copies of the lyrics to "Take Your Gun and Go, John" (below) and distribute to each team.

2. Have teams use **Team Investigation** to read the lyrics and list ways that the war will affect the home front.

3. Elicit that the speaker in the song lives on a farm. Have teams change the lyrics so they apply to families of factory workers, merchants, teachers, restaurant owners, and others.

4. Use **Numbered Heads** to discuss how the war affects the home front, and **Timed Telling** to have teams share their rewritten lyrics.

Don't stop a moment to think, John;
Our country calls, then go.
Don't fear for me nor the children, John,
I'll care for them, you know!
Leave the corn upon the stock, John:
The fruit upon the tree,
And all our little stores, John:
Yes leave them all to me.

(Chorus) *Then take your gun and go,*
Yes, take your gun and go,
For Ruth can drive the oxen, John,
And I can use the hoe.

The army's short of blankets, John,
Then take this heavy pair,
I spun and wove them when a girl,
And worked them with great care,
A rose in every corner, John;
And here's my name, you see!

On the cold ground they'll warmer feel,
Because they're made by me. Chorus

And, John, if God has willed it so
We ne'er shall meet again,
I'll do the best for the children, John,
In sorrow, want or pain,
On winter nights I'll teach them, John,
All that I learned at school:
To love our country, keep her laws
Obey the Savior's rule. Chorus

And now good-bye to you, John;
I cannot say Farewell!
We'll hope and pray for the best, John;
His goodness none can tell,
May His arm be round about you, John,
To guard you night and day;
Be our beloved country's shield,
Till war shall pass away.

ASSESSMENT

SUMMARIZING PART 3

Part 3 Check-Up   Use Check-Up 3 (TG page 95) to assess student learning in Part 3.

ALTERNATE ASSESSMENT

Ask students to write an essay answering one of the following questions, which link the big ideas across chapters:

1. Making Connections   Many different kinds of conflicts are mentioned in Part 3. Name some of these conflicts, and identify the issues involved. *(Answers will vary. To get students started, you might give an example: conflict over secession/states' rights vs. federalism or personal conflicts like Robert E. Lee's decision to turn down the leadership of the Northern army.)*

2. Making Connections   Discuss how this saying by Lincoln might have been good advice for both the North and South at the start of the war: "The hen is the wisest of all the animal creation, because she never cackles until after the egg is laid." *(Possible response: Neither side should boast of victory until the war was won.)*

DEBATING THE ISSUES
Use the topic below to stimulate debate.

Resolved   That Abraham Lincoln should at the beginning of hostilities establish abolition as the goal of war. (To stimulate debate, appoint several students to speak for abolitionists such as William Seward, Frederick Douglass, Harriet Tubman, or Sojourner Truth. Have others represent the views of Lincoln or Ulysses S. Grant—who had to make sure soldiers supported the war.)

MAKING ETHICAL JUDGMENTS
The following activity asks students to consider issues of ethics.

Robert E. Lee loved both the Union and his native state. Unlike his father, however, Lee chose to support Virginia. Imagine you are Lee on the night of his terrible decision to turn down Lincoln's offer to lead the Union army. Write a letter to your children, explaining why you did not follow in your father's footsteps. Make sure students use the word *honor* in their explanations. (Request students to read their letters aloud. Ask volunteers to explain what decision they would have made.)

PROJECTS AND ACTIVITIES
Making a Chart   Students can work in small groups to design charts that list the advantages or disadvantages of the North and South at the start of the Civil War. Categories for comparison should include: military, political, economic, geographic, leadership, other. Ask students to study their charts, then ask which side they think would take an early lead in the war.

USING THE RUBRICS

To assess these writing assignments, group projects, and activities, scoring rubrics have been provided at the back of this Teaching Guide. Be sure to explain the rubrics to your students.

LOOKING AHEAD

Analyzing a Quote

Shortly after Lincoln issued a call for troops, an eighteen-year-old West Point cadet wrote to his fiancée:

> *There is a certain hymn that is always sung...the last Sunday that graduates attend church here. It commences "When shall we meet again?"...And everyone felt the truth of the concluding words, "Never, no more," for in all probability in another year, the half of them may be in their graves.*

Ask students what insights this quote gives them into the personal nature of the war. Use their remarks to lead into Part 4.

Writing an Ad   Before assigning Chapters 12 and 13, have students write an advertisement for the ideal generals to lead both the Confederate and Union armies. Which soldier described in the two chapters best fits this description?

Mapping a War   Students should be creating their personal overview map of the Civil War using the Civil War reproduible map. Extend this activity by creating a large wall map of the United States on which to plot the course of war. Students can begin by labeling Union, Confederate, and border states. (See the map on page 67.) As they continue to read Book Six, students can label battle sites and other key places.

Analyzing a Quote   Repeat the remark by the Confederate soldier on page 68: "I'd rather die than become a slave to the North." Challenge students to create monologues in which they explain what the soldier meant by this remark, especially the use of the word *slave.*

Designing a Political Cartoon   Assign groups of students to draw political cartoons that capture problems faced by Jefferson Davis under government by a confederation. You might also assign several groups to create a cartoon expressing the Southern view of a republic controlled by Northerners.

THE BIG IDEAS

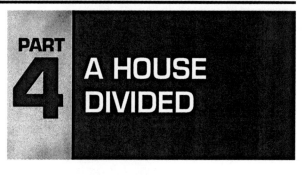

It was not only presidents and generals who faced wrenching decisions as the nation went to war. In May 1861, Cherokee leader John Ross fired off a letter to the nearest Union fort. He feared that the warring states might try to drag Native Americans into the conflict. Wrote Ross:

> *The Cherokees have properly taken no part in the present deplorable state of affairs....We do not wish our soil to become the battle ground between the states, and our home to be rendered desolate and miserable by the horrors of a civil war.*

CHAPTERS 15–17
15 Choosing Sides 76
16 The Soldiers 80
17 Willie and Tad 86

But it proved impossible to stay out of the conflict. Eventually Ross gave in and signed an agreement with the South when slave-owning Cherokee wanted to join the Confederacy. But other members of the Five Civilized Tribes could not forgive the South for its role in their removal from their homeland. They appealed to President Lincoln for help. Soon blue and gray troops headed across the Mississippi, spreading the conflict of civil war to all Native Americans including the Cherokee. Part 4 describes the heartbreaking decisions that split families and people apart.

INTRODUCING PART 4

SETTING GOALS

Introduce Part 4 by asking: "When studying a war, is it more important to study battles and strategy or how individual soldiers felt and lived?" (*Answers will vary, but lead students to understand that no war is really understood without looking at what the average soldier went through. This is the focus of Part 4.*)

To set goals for Part 4, tell students that they will
- describe the attitudes and attributes of Northern and Southern soldiers.
- evaluate how well old strategies were suited for the new weapons.
- empathize with Lincoln and understand how his family was a source of comfort and grief during the war.

SETTING A CONTEXT FOR READING

Thinking About the Big Ideas   Write the title of Chapter 15—*Choosing Sides*—on the chalkboard. Have students think of times they've had to choose sides between friends. It's hard to stay out of the conflict, especially when each friend wants support. Use this analogy to talk about the difficult choice people had to make during the Civil War. Read aloud the quotation from John Ross at the beginning of this introduction. Ask students what Ross' reaction to the Civil War was, and whether the Cherokee's neutrality in Oklahoma was threatened. (Point out on a map that Oklahoma bordered on the Confederacy.)

Reading with Empathy For most young people the idea of fighting in a war seems unreal. Yet many of the soldiers on both sides were very young. Discuss with students if they would ever volunteer to fight in a war today. (*Many might say they would only fight if family or friends were threatened. Others might say the idea of war sounds exciting.*) Try to connect your students' responses to what they are about to read in Part 4. Encourage them to see these young soldiers as similar to themselves.

SETTING A CONTEXT IN SPACE AND TIME

Linking Geography and War On the opening page of Chapter 15 (page 76), the author says, "Most men went to war for their region." You might begin Part 4 by having students review the definition of *region.* (*a place or group of places linked by similar characteristics*) Then make a Venn diagram on the chalkboard. Label the left circle *North* and the right circle *South.* Label the overlapping part *U.S.*

In the center, list with students some of the common characteristics and shared beliefs that define the United States. Then, in the sections labeled *North* and *South,* list traits that defined each of these regions. Have students use this diagram to describe how regionalism helped pull the United States apart. When Southerners went to war, what were they fighting for? What were Northerners fighting for? Encourage students to modify the diagram as they progress through the rest of the book.

Understanding Historical Benchmarks Explain to students that the term *benchmark* originally referred to the mark a surveyor put on a permanent landmark of a known altitude. Surveyors used the benchmark to help them determine elevations of other points. Next, tell students that the Civil War is an important benchmark in U.S. history. Ask students why this period can be considered a permanent landmark from which to measure the ups and downs of liberty, national unity, and equality. (If students have difficulty with this concept, suggest that they look backward from 1861. What would they see? Then have them look forward from the end of the war. What changes in American life do they expect to see?)

CHAPTER 15

CHOOSING SIDES

PAGES 76–79

1 Class Period   **Homework: Student Study Guide p. 23**

Chapter Summary

Like all civil wars, the American Civil War was a complicated mess of families fighting families, and friends fighting friends. However, most soldiers knew they were fighting for a way of life. The Northern way of democracy, liberty, and free (non-slave) labor triumphed.

Key Vocabulary

pastoral	class society
antebellum	democracy

1. CONNECT

Remind students of Robert E. Lee's difficult choice between his country and his state (Chapter 13). Explain that other soldiers were also torn. Just as the Revolution forced people to choose sides, the Civil War sometimes split families. Ask students what they would do were they to come face-to-face with their best friend in battle.

2. UNDERSTAND

1. Read pages 76-77 up to "They were to meet again...." Discuss: The author begins the chapter with several examples of relatives and friends forced apart by the war. Which of the examples do you find most interesting and powerful?

2. Read the rest of the chapter. Ask: What are some of the ways in which Northern and Southern life differed? (*North: urban, industrial, no slaves, greater social mobility; South: rural, agricultural, slaves, less social mobility*) According to the author, did the Civil War make a difference? How so? (*It ended slavery, preserved the Union, and the U.S. Constitution was amended to protect equality of opportunity and fairness for all.*)

3. CHECK UNDERSTANDING

Writing   Have students write a letter as a Northern soldier explaining to their brother (who has joined the Confederacy) their choice to join the Union cause. Students should use specific details from the chapter to make their letters more powerful.

Thinking About the Chapter (Analyzing)   Ask students to analyze the difference between the causes of a war and reasons individuals choose to fight. (*Lead students to understand that although slavery, preserving the Union, and states' rights may have triggered the war, most individual soldiers were fighting for glory, or as the author says, for a way of life.*)

READING NONFICTION

Analyzing Text Organization

Have students identify the main idea of this chapter. Ask: What is the author's main argument? (*that the war split families as well as the nation*) Where is it stated? (*in the first two sentences*) Then ask partners to skim the text and note how each paragraph gives information supporting the main idea.

LINKING DISCIPLINES

History/Photography

The Civil War was the first heavily photographed war in U.S. history. Have students examine the photographs of soldiers throughout the chapter. Discuss the poses, dress, and equipment. Ask interested students to find out why there are no action photographs of the Civil War. They can research Mathew Brady and the history of photography to find out. An interesting article about Brady and his photography business can be found at *www.photo-seminars.com/Fame/mathew.htm.*

READING NONFICTION

Analyzing Graphic Aids

Ask students to identify the theme of the pictures on page 83-85. (*All show new technologies used in the war.*) Then ask students to debate which innovations they think had the most impact on the war, and why new technologies are often developed or improved during times of war. (*to gain advantage over an enemy*)

LINKING DISCIPLINES

History/Food

Have students research the recipe for hardtack, the staple food of soldiers during the war. There are many recipes. A number can be found at *www.geocities.com/Pentagon/Barracks/1369/ recipes.html*. Have them write down the recipe and bake a pan of hardtack for the class. Bon appetit!

ACTIVITIES/JOHNS HOPKINS TEAM LEARNING

See the Student Team Learning Activity on TG page 64.

MORE ABOUT...

Civil War Casualties

The prison camps set up by both sides to hold prisoners of war were as deadly as any battle. The worst POW camp was Andersonville, a Confederate camp in Georgia. Historians estimate that over 13,700 Union prisoners died of disease, starvation, and neglect there. In 1970, Andersonville was declared a national historic site and it is now the home of the National Prisoner of War Museum.

CHAPTER 16 THE SOLDIERS

PAGES 80-85

1 Class Period   Homework: Student Study Guide p. 24

Chapter Summary

At first, the armies tried to fight the Civil War according to old lessons learned at West Point. But new weapons had rewritten the rules of war. Rapid-fire guns and modern artillery turned battlefields into smoke-filled bloodbaths. As the warfare spilled into civilian areas, Americans saw the horrors of total war.

Key Vocabulary

conscription	draft	sloosh
hardtack	breech loading	total war

1. CONNECT

The theme of technology changing the way we do things is central to American history. Tell students that technology often changes faster than people's attitudes about the technology. Elicit from students how this would affect how armies wage war. (*Generals might be slow to adapt and casualties might result.*)

2. UNDERSTAND

1. Read pages 80-82. Discuss: Describe the average recruit in both the North and South. (*a farmer or small town man of 24 or younger*) Why did joining the army seem like an exciting thing to do in 1861? (*Life was much slower, full of work, and there was little travel and recreation available.*)
2. Read the rest of the chapter. Ask: Why was the Civil War more deadly than previous wars? (*New weapons caused terrible casualties, and the war expanded beyond the battlefield, creating total war.*) Why did the old military strategies fail? (*Long-range weapons and use of trenches changed the rules of war.*)
3. Graphs: For a closer look at some interesting statistics of the war, have students complete Resource Page 6 (TG page 110).

3. CHECK UNDERSTANDING

Writing   Have students write a paragraph supporting the idea that the Civil War is called the first modern war. They should give at least three reasons. They should also use and define the term *total war*.

Thinking About the Chapter (Evaluating)   Have students review the changes that Civil War generals had to adapt to. List the changes on the board in two columns: *Technology* (such as weaponry) and *Human* (such as fighting spirit). Have students evaluate the relative importance of each item listed. They can return to the list to make changes as they read the rest of Book 6.

17 WILLIE AND TAD

PAGES 86–88

1 Class Period   **Homework: Student Study Guide p. 25**

Chapter Summary
Lincoln tried to escape the pain of civil war in the shelter of his family. But criticism of his wife, Mary Todd Lincoln, and the death of one of his sons made Lincoln's life almost unbearable.

Key Vocabulary
compassion   hayseed

1. CONNECT

Ask students to tell what they know about the current president's family. Ask them if they feel it is important for Americans to know our president "up close and personal."

2. UNDERSTAND

1. Read the chapter. Discuss: The author describes Abraham Lincoln as a man of compassion. What does this mean, and why did the Civil War take such an emotional toll on Lincoln? (*His compassion led him to feel the suffering of others.*)
2. What personal tragedies increased Lincoln's woe? (*He endured criticisms of his wife and the death of one of his sons.*)

3. CHECK UNDERSTANDING

Writing   Have students write a one-page diary entry as if they were either Mary Lincoln, Tad Lincoln, or a White House servant during the Civil War. Make sure they discuss their feelings about living in the White House and their opinion of how the war is affecting the President.

Thinking About the Chapter (Evaluating)   Lead the class in a discussion about why the author included an entire chapter on Lincoln's family life during the war. (*It is interesting and it helps humanize Lincoln.*) Go further by discussing with students why it is important to portray even our heroes as human beings who suffer, love, and make mistakes.

MEETING INDIVIDUAL NEEDS

Below-level readers may find the story of Willie and Tad a more manageable topic than the more complicated subjects of Gettysburg or slavery. Have these students present the information in Chapter 17 to the class. This chance at being an expert might build confidence for some of the more difficult activities and readings in the upcoming chapters.

JOHNS HOPKINS TEAM LEARNING

CHILDREN AT WAR

JOHNS HOPKINS
U N I V E R S I T Y

1 CLASS PERIOD

FOCUS ACTIVITY

1. Ask students what their major daily concerns are. List some on the chalkboard.

2. Brainstorm what the concerns of children during wartime might be. If students have read about children caught in the Bosnian civil war in the 1990s, elicit what they know.

STUDENT TEAM LEARNING ACTIVITY/USING HISTORICAL IMAGINATION

1. Divide the class into teams of four. Distribute to teams the quotations below from children who participated in the Civil War.

2. Team members should take turns reading the quotations aloud, and then use **Round Robin** to express how they would feel or what they would do in such a situation.

3. Bring the class together to draw conclusions about the effects of war on children.

*A ball [bullet] hit my drum and bounced off and I fell over. When I got up, another ball tore a hole in the drum and another came so close to my ear that I heard it sing.—*Confederate drummer boy, Virginia

*My daddy go away to the war bout this time, and my mammy and me stay in our cabin alone. She cry and wonder where he be, if he is well or he be killed, and one day we hear he is dead. My mammy, too, pass in a short time.—*Annie Lumpkin, former slave, South Carolina

*We are starving. As soon as enough of us get together we are going to take the bakeries and each of us will take a loaf of bread. This is little enough for the government to give us after it has taken all our men.—*Young Southern girl, Richmond, Virginia

*The church yard was strewn with arms and legs that had been amputated and thrown out the windows, and all around were wounded men for whom no place had yet been found.—*Charles McCurdy, 10, Gettysburg, Pennsylvania

*I want to say, as we lay there and the shells were flying over us, my thoughts went back to my home, and I thought what a foolish boy I was to run away and get into such a mess as I was in. I would have been glad to have seen my father coming after me.—*Elisha Stockwell, Jr., 15, Wisconsin

*When the recruiting officer asked my age, I told him the truth. "I am sixteen next June," I said....The officer ordered me out of line and my father, who was behind me, stepped up to the table. "He can work as steady as any man," my father explained. "And he can shoot as straight as any who has been signed today. I am the boy's father."...the officer handed me the pen and ordered, "Sign here."—*Ned Hunter, 15, Mississippi

*...suddenly a shell came down on top of the hill...and exploded. This caused a large mass of earth to slide...catching me under it. Dr. Lord, whose leg was caught and held by it, gave the alarm that a child was buried. Mother reached me first, and...succeeded in getting my head out first....They pulled me from under the mass of earth. The blood was gushing from my nose, eyes, ears, and mouth...but there were no bones broken.—*Lucy McRae, a young Southern girl, Vicksburg

*I passed...the corpse of a beautiful boy in gray....He was clad in a bright and neat uniform, well garnished with gold, which seemed to tell the story of a loving mother and sisters who had sent their household pet to the field of war. His neat little hat lying beside him bore the number of a Georgia regiment....He was about my age....At the sight of the poor boy's corpse, I burst into a regular boo-hoo and started on.—*John Cockerill, 16, Union regimental musician

ASSESSMENT

Part 4 Check-Up   Use Check-Up 4 (TG page 96) to assess student learning in Part 4.

ALTERNATE ASSESSMENT
Ask students to complete one of the following activities, which link the big ideas across chapters.

1. Making Connections   Divide the class into four groups: Northern soldiers before the war, Southern soldiers before the war, Northern soldiers after fighting a battle involving modern weapons, Southern soldiers after fighting a battle involving modern weapons. Each group should write a skit in which the soldiers talk about their attitudes concerning the war. They should all use information from the text that refers to attitude, soldiering life, weapons, etc. (It is important for students to see that as new technologies made the war more deadly, the bravado and excitement of war lessened.) You may wish to have students practice and perform their skits.

2. Making Connections   Have students write an essay in which they discuss why the typical Civil War soldier was so unprepared for "total war." (*Few were trained soldiers and the methods and weapons were different from those of any previous conflict.*)

DEBATING THE ISSUES
Use the topic below to stimulate debate.

Resolved   That Tad Lincoln was right: the Union should hang on to the Rebels. (Tell the students that from the minute the war started, Northerners discussed whether to allow the Confederacy to leave and end the war. Others wanted to crush the South into submission and keep them there so they could not rise again. Have some students take Tad's moderate view. Appoint others to adopt a punitive view.)

MAKING ETHICAL JUDGMENTS
The following activities ask students to consider issues of ethics.

1. Remind students of the number of young people below the age of eighteen who enlisted for service in the Civil War. Divide the class into small groups. Then ask each group to develop a dialogue in which a teenager tells family members why he or she must head off to war. (The young person can be from the North or South. The recruit might be male or female: see "The Odyssey of Pvt. Rosetta Wakeman, Union Army" in the January 1994 issue of *American Heritage*. Tell students to be sure to cite the ethical reasons for their decision.)

2. Engage the class in a discussion about the saying "A rich man's war and a poor man's fight." Ask students if it was fair that a Northerner who was drafted could pay a substitute to take his

USING THE RUBRICS

To assess these writing assignments, group projects, and activities, scoring rubrics have been provided at the back of this Teaching Guide. Be sure to explain the rubrics to your students.

Comparing Quotes

Read aloud the following quotations:

> *It is well that war is so terrible, or we should grow too fond of it.*
>
> Robert E. Lee, Battle
> of Fredericksburg, 1862

> *It is only those who have neither fired a shot nor heard the shrieks and groans of the wounded who cry aloud for blood, more vengeance, more desolation. War is hell.*
>
> William T. Sherman, Address at
> Michigan Military Academy, 1879

Ask students what the quotations have in common. (*Both convey an understanding of the brutality of war.*) What can students infer about the battles they will soon study? (*They were horrible, full of courage and destruction.*)

place. This usually cost about $300. To enrich the discussion, remind students that nobody forced substitutes to take the money. Ask: If the nation was at war today and you were drafted, would you pay for a substitute if you could?

PROJECTS AND ACTIVITIES

Writing a Diary   Assign students to write diary entries for some of the young soldiers pictured in the text photos: William Presgraves, Edwin Francis Jennison, Johnny Clem. At least two entries should capture the flavor of camp life. Another two entries should reveal the horrors of modern war.

Representing Information Visually   Assign to groups or individuals a poster project entitled *One Nation, Two Societies*. Explain that each poster should have two equal frames. One frame should capture the way of life in the North. The other frame should portray the way of life in the South. Display these posters in the classroom, and refer to them at the end of the book. Ask students how the war changed each of the two frames.

Analyzing a Political Cartoon   Refer students to the cartoon on page 79. Tell them to imagine they are Abraham Lincoln. How might they respond to the cartoon? (Encourage students to refer to Part 3 for comments on Lincoln's distinction between slavery and those who practiced it.) After this discussion, have students write a letter to the editor in which Lincoln reacts to the cartoonist's point of view.

THE BIG IDEAS

On January 1, 1863, Abraham Lincoln signed the Emancipation Proclamation. Ralph Waldo Emerson immediately grasped the importance of the event. Declared Emerson:

The force of the act is that it commits the country to…justice.…Done it cannot be undone.…The…act makes clear that the lives of our heroes have not been sacrificed in vain. It makes a victory of our defeats. Our hurts are healed. The health of the nation is repaired.

Frederick Douglass put the matter more simply: "The act has thrown a moral bombshell in the Confederacy." Part 5 describes the conflicts on the battlefield and the act that made sense of the sacrifices.

CHAPTERS 18–26
18 General McClellan's Campaign 89
19 War at Sea 94
20 Emancipation Means Freedom 98
21 Determined Soldiers 103
22 Marching Soldiers 107
23 Awesome Fighting 111
24 Lee the Fox 117
25 Speeches at Gettysburg 119
26 More Battles—Will It Ever End? 124

INTRODUCING PART 5

SETTING GOALS

Introduce Part 5 by writing on the board, "The ends justify the means." Elicit the meaning of the phrase and review the concept of total war. Ask the class if they feel that total destruction of an enemy—including noncombatants—is justified in wartime. What if it is to end slavery and preserve the Union?

To set goals for Part 5, tell students that they will
• assess the performance of Union and Confederate commanders and troops.
• discuss the Emancipation Proclamation and the Gettysburg address.
• identify and describe the turning point of the war (Gettysburg, Vicksburg).

SETTING A CONTEXT FOR READING

Thinking About the Big Ideas   Read aloud Lincoln's statement of Union goals in the Introduction to Part 3 (TG page 50). Then read the passage from the Emancipation Proclamation on page 98. Ask students how the goals of the war had changed. Discuss the effect the proclamation would have had on the morale of Northern soldiers tired of being beaten by Southern armies. Lead students to understand how sacrifice in the name of liberty boosted morale.

Memorizing Important Passages   Although memorizing an excerpt from a great speech may seem difficult to students, it adds to their respect and understanding of it. Ask your students to memorize Lincoln's Gettysburg Address in Chapter 25 (or source #53 in *A History of US Sourcebook*). Tell them it is only about 270 words, but they are all good words, and they changed the course of history.

SETTING A CONTEXT IN SPACE AND TIME

Researching the Geography of War   Have students choose a battle other than Gettysburg and research the geography of the battle. Ask them to look closely at two things: the movement of the soldiers during the battle, and the terrain and its impact on the course of the battle. Have them create a model or diorama of the battle and present it to the class.

Creating an Annotated Time Line   Have students create a time line of major Civil War battles. Time lines should be annotated with important points about each battle. Students should create a symbol for each battle. For example, Manassas (Bull Run) might be represented by a picnic basket; Gettysburg could be symbolized by a U-turn sign signifying the turning point of the war.

18 GENERAL McCLELLAN'S CAMPAIGN

PAGES 89-93

1 Class Period   Homework: Student Study Guide p. 26

Chapter Summary
When the Civil War opened, Confederate generals such as Stonewall Jackson ran circles around Union commander George McClellan. The cautious-minded Union general never struck a great blow at the South. The greatest blow came instead when a stray Confederate bullet caused Jackson's death.

Key Vocabulary
campaign   peninsula   ruse

1. CONNECT

Have students recall what they know of General McClellan from Chapter 12. *(cautious, slow, leader of Union forces after the first battle of Bull Run)* McClellan's campaign was his effort to capture Richmond. Have students predict what may happen.

2. UNDERSTAND

1. Read pages 89-90 up to "First, there was McClellan himself." Discuss: How did McClellan help get the Union army back on its feet after Bull Run? What was his war plan? *(He brought order, discipline, pride, food, and equipment to his army. He planned on surrounding Richmond and squeezing the South.)*
2. Read the rest of the chapter. What obstacles worked against his plan? *(McClellan's lack of decisiveness, excessive rain, and Confederate generals such as Stonewall Jackson and John Magruder.)*
3. Evaluate with students which side was "winning" in the early years of the Civil War. *(Although it seemed to be a draw, the South had the advantage, for they only had to outlast the North's will to fight.)*

3. CHECK UNDERSTANDING

Writing   Most people who are fired from their jobs are given reasons. After McClellan's failed campaign, Lincoln relieved him of his command. Have students write a letter of dismissal from Lincoln to McClellan explaining in detail his reasons.

Thinking About the Chapter (Categorizing)   With students, complete a two-column chart of reasons why the Peninsula campaign failed. Categorize the reasons as *Under McClellan's Control* and *Beyond McClellan's Control*. Then have students evaluate whether the Peninsula campaign could have been successful at that time of the war.

READING NONFICTION
Analyzing Primary and Secondary Sources
Have students identify the primary and secondary sources in the sidebars. (*All are primary except for the excerpt from* Stonewall.) Ask partners to record a memorable phrase or image from each source that helps them understand what was happening.

GEOGRAPHY CONNECTIONS
Civil War Room Activity
Have students continue the Civil War Room activity as described on TG page 26. Have them locate and mark the following:

McClellan's Campaign

Richmond	37°30'N 77°22W
Petersburg	37°07'N 77°22'W
James River	
Chancellorsville	38°15'N 77°37'W

GEOGRAPHY CONNECTIONS

Civil War Room Activity

Have students continue the Civil War Room activity as described on TG page 26. Have them locate and mark the following:

Location of the "Battle of the Ironclads"

Hampton Roads	37°00'N 76°15'W
Norfolk	36°52'N 76°15'W
New Orleans	30°00'N 90°00'W
Mississippi River	
Atlantic Ocean	

Help students understand why Stanton and other people in Washington D.C. were so scared by the *Virginia*'s first success. (*It was a short sail for the "indestructible ship" from Hampton Roads to Washington.*)

Have students identify the site of the battle of the ironclads and of Farragut's exploits on Resource Page 1 (TG page 99).

LINKING DISCIPLINES

Technology/Weapons

An exciting project is to research and build a model of either the *Virginia* or the *Monitor* and present it to the class. Have students explain the design of the ships and discuss with the class the obstacles the engineers had to overcome to build them.

CHAPTER 19 — WAR AT SEA

PAGES 94–97

1 Class Period   Homework: Student Study Guide p. 27

Chapter Summary

While soldiers handled new weapons on land, the first ironclad ships prowled the Chesapeake Bay. The *Virginia (Merrimack)* and the *Monitor* foreshadowed the great steel fleets of the future. At the same time, David Farragut was winning decisive naval victories to take control of the Mississippi River.

Key Vocabulary

ironclads

1. CONNECT

Remind students that they have already studied the impact of changing technology on warfare in Chapter 16. This chapter focuses on a famous battle between two ironclad ships. The age of wooden, sail-powered navies was about to come to an end.

2. UNDERSTAND

1. Read the chapter. Discuss: How did the *Virginia* and the *Monitor* revolutionize naval warfare? (*Their iron armor made wooden ships vulnerable and obsolete.*) Have students describe the battle between the two ironclads. (*It was a draw that lasted 4 hours; cannonballs bounced off the sides of each ship.*)
2. Read the feature Ruler of the President's Navy. Ask: What was David Farragut's contribution to the Civil War? (*He was a Southerner who commanded the Union ships that helped capture New Orleans and the Mississippi River.*)

3. CHECK UNDERSTANDING

Writing   Have students imagine they are Secretary of War Stanton and write two diary entries. The first should be for the day Stanton received news of the *Virginia*'s appearance. The second should be a reaction after the battle between the *Monitor* and the *Virginia*.

Thinking About the Chapter (Making Judgments)   Note with students that the chapter is divided into two sections: the ironclads and David Farragut. Have students decide which would be likely to have a greater effect on the Civil War, and which would be likely to have a greater long-term effect. (*Students should use the details to ascertain that the capture of New Orleans and control of the Mississippi probably had a greater effect on the outcome of the Civil War, whereas the battle of the ironclads changed the future of navies.*)

CHAPTER 20 — EMANCIPATION MEANS FREEDOM

PAGES 98-102

1 Class Period   Homework: Student Study Guide p. 28

Chapter Summary

The South called the Civil War a revolution. But it took the Emancipation Proclamation to turn the conflict into a true revolution. With this act, Lincoln made it clear that slavery would end if the Union won the Civil War.

Key Vocabulary

Emancipation Proclamation

1. CONNECT

Recall John Brown's words just before he died, "I…am now quite certain that the sins of this guilty land will never be purged away, but with blood." In this chapter students will read about this purging, including the bloodiest day of the war and the document that changed the meaning of the war.

2. UNDERSTAND

1. Read pages 98-99. Have students explain why Antietam was both a great victory and a missed opportunity for the Union. (*Lee's army was stopped, but McClellan let Lee escape.*)
2. Read the rest of the chapter. Discuss: The author suggests that the war began to change attitudes of people in the North, including Lincoln. Explain. (*Northerners began to realize that all their sacrifice would be in vain if slavery was allowed to continue.*) How did the Emancipation Proclamation change the purpose of the war? (*It declared abolition of slavery in the South, in addition to the preservation of the Union, as a clear goal of the North.*)

3. CHECK UNDERSTANDING

Writing Ask students to write a paragraph explaining the following quote on page 100. "Today, when you think about it, it doesn't sound as if Lincoln really did much [when he issued the Emancipation Proclamation]. People in 1862 knew differently."

Thinking About the Chapter (Drawing Conclusions) The author argues that Lincoln did not free slaves in the border states because he did not have the constitutional authority to do so. Discuss some other reasons. (*He was fearful of losing support in these already tenuous states.*) Was this a good decision to keep thousands of people in slavery for two more years in order to win the war?

READING NONFICTION

Analyzing Rhetorical Devices

Discuss that speeches present good opportunities for using rhetoric, or stylistic elements such as repetition, unusual syntax or word choices, that emphasize the speakers' ideas. Ask partners to list rhetorical elements they find in Lincoln's and Douglass' speeches (pages 98 and 100). Then have them rewrite one speech in everyday language to share with the class. Afterward, discuss what is lost or gained by the rewriting.

GEOGRAPHY CONNECTIONS

Civil War Room Activity

Have students continue the Civil War Room activity as described on TG page 26. Have them locate and mark the following:

Antietam (Sharpsburg)   39°22'N 77°37'W

Then have students identify the areas on the map where the Emancipation Proclamation freed slaves.

MEETING INDIVIDUAL NEEDS

You may wish to have students watch the first 10 minutes of the movie *Glory*, which portrays the courage and chaos of the desperate Battle of Antietam.

MORE ABOUT…

Diplomacy

Lincoln hoped the Emancipation Proclamation would keep the antislavery British from entering the war on the side of the South. It had the desired effect. The British could not justify fighting against a side that was attempting to end a practice outlawed and condemned in Britain for decades.

READING NONFICTION

Analyzing Point of View

Discuss that readers usually have an easy time learning what author Joy Hakim thinks about a subject—her voice is often loud and clear. Ask: What words in the first paragraph on page 103 state her opinion of prejudice? (*dumb, idiotic, stupid*) How else does she support her point of view? (*Students should point out other phrases, and notice that all of her statements support the idea that black people were good soldiers.*)

MORE ABOUT...

Black Soldiers

By the end of the war black soldiers made up nearly 10 percent of the Union Army. Sergeant William Carney, in the assault on Fort Wagner, was shot five times and still managed to carry the flag back to the Union lines. Twenty years later, he was rewarded with the Medal of Honor for his actions.

GEOGRAPHY CONNECTIONS

Civil War Room Activity

Have students continue the Civil War Room activity as described on TG page 26. Have them locate and mark the following:

Fort Wagner (Charleston)   32°45'N 79°52'W

CHAPTER 21 DETERMINED SOLDIERS

PAGES 103-106

1 Class Period   **Homework: Student Study Guide p. 29**

Chapter Summary

Because of prejudice in the North, black men were initially denied the right to fight in the Civil War. However, the heroism and valor of black troops, like the Massachusetts 54th Regiment, led to what one reporter called "a revolution [of] the public mind."

Key Vocabulary

contraband

1. CONNECT

If students have seen the movie *Glory*, begin discussion by eliciting details they remember from the movie. (The movie is about the Massachusetts 54th regiment and their attack on Fort Wagner.) Ask: If a person has risked his life for his country, can he be denied the rights granted to others who risked their lives?

2. UNDERSTAND

1. Read pages 103-104. Discuss: Why didn't the Union armies allow African Americans to enlist early in the war? (*Prejudice and fear were strong in much of the North.*) How were enslaved blacks forced to contribute to the Confederate war effort? (*They had to do the work and grow the food needed by the Confederate armies.*)
2. Read the rest of the chapter. Ask: How did the 54th Massachusetts turn Northern ideas about black soldiers upside down? (*It showed that black troops could fight bravely and well.*)
3. Ask: What did Abraham Lincoln mean when he said, "In giving freedom to the slave, we assure freedom to the free"? (*Students may interpret Lincoln's words as meaning that so long as slavery exists, a society can never be totally free.*)

3. CHECK UNDERSTANDING

Writing Have students write a journal entry as if they were the soldiers in the pictures in the chapter. Their entries should focus on why they are fighting and what the experience means to them. Students should incorporate details from the chapter in their entries.

Thinking About the Chapter (Analyzing) Have students explain why black soldiers had to prove themselves in battle to gain acceptance. (*prejudice in the North, disbelief about their abilities, old opinions are hard to break*) Why did it take special courage for black soldiers to fight the Confederates? (*If they were captured, they would be sold into slavery or killed.*)

22 MARCHING SOLDIERS

PAGES 107–110

1 Class Period   **Homework: Student Study Guide p. 30**

Chapter Summary

Generals began to realize that anything they could do to weaken the enemy would help win the war. This realization opened the door to total war and expanded the misery of the civilian population of the South. Chapter 22 sets the stage for the pivotal battle at Gettysburg.

Key Vocabulary

hardtack   total war

1. CONNECT

Write these adjectives on the chalkboard: *conservative, daring, courageous, fearful, patient, gambler*. Have the class choose three adjectives describing traits they would want a general in their army to have. *Daring, courageous,* and *gambler* are all words used to describe Robert E. Lee, and never more than when he decided to invade the North in the summer of 1863.

2. UNDERSTAND

1. Read pages 107-108 up to "Mostly it was the South...." Discuss: How and why did the Union bring total war to the South? (*Union soldiers fed and housed themselves on whatever the land had to offer, and destroyed property to keep it from being used against them. Making life difficult for civilians would weaken the South.*)
2. Read the rest of the chapter. Why did Lee invade the North? (*He believed Northerners might seek peace if the Confederates beat them on their own ground. That is, they would have a glimpse of the suffering that war could bring.*)

3. CHECK UNDERSTANDING

Writing   Have students imagine that they are Northerners who have just read about Lee's invasion in 1863. Have them write a paragraph describing their feelings and what they believe Lee is trying to accomplish.

Thinking About the Chapter (Evaluating Author's Purpose)

Discuss with students the contrast that the author sets up in this chapter: total war (and the past geologic cataclysm) with the idyllic nature of Gettysburg. Ask: Why does she use this contrast? (*Total war is coming to an area of the North, which had previously been untouched by the war. The chapter creates expectancy of a great battle, possibly the most important of the war.*)

READING NONFICTION

Analyzing Graphic Aids

Have students find the compass rose and use the map key to help them locate the position of Union and Confederate forces. Ask: Which forces occupied part of the town of Gettysburg? (*Confederate*) Were the Union troops east or west of the Confederate position? (*east*) Did Pickett's Charge come from the north or west? (*west*) Which side had more natural protection? Why? (*Union; they were defending high ground.*)

MEETING INDIVIDUAL NEEDS

Gettysburg is a very complicated three-day battle. Visual learners will benefit from creating a ten-step flow chart of key events in the battle. They should clearly delineate each day within the diagram.

GEOGRAPHY CONNECTIONS

Civil War Room Activity

Have students continue the Civil War Room activity as described on TG page 26. Have them locate and mark the following:

Gettysburg   39°45'N 77°07'W

CHAPTER 23 AWESOME FIGHTING

PAGES 111-116

1 Class Period   **Homework: Student Study Guide p. 30**

Chapter Summary

Gettysburg was a three-day battle that turned the tide of the war. The gallantry and carnage of these three days are forever seared on the national memory. In a daring move, Lee gambled everything on an old-fashioned military charge. When the gamble failed, it left the South unable to ever again threaten Northern territory.

Key Vocabulary

cavalry

1. CONNECT

Discuss what a turning point is. Ask students if they can identify a personal turning point, something that changed the direction of their life and helped shape them as a person. Note that such moments can be positive or negative for different people, as the Battle of Gettysburg was.

2. UNDERSTAND

1. Read pages 111-112. Discuss: In what ways was fighting at Gettysburg accidental? (*Nobody planned to fight there. Rebel troops headed there to look for shoes and happened to meet Union troops. It was a "good location for a fight."*)
2. Map: Have students complete Resource Page 7 (TG page 111) to examine how the area's topography influenced the battle's outcome.
3. Read the rest of the chapter. Discuss: What was Pickett's Charge, and why did it fail? (*It was an old-fashioned military charge across open fields. The Confederate cannons did not destroy the Union lines, and the massed Rebel troops were easy targets for the Union troops who were waiting behind walls.*)

3. CHECK UNDERSTANDING

Writing   Have teams of students write a newspaper account of the Battle of Gettysburg from either a Northern or Southern perspective. Make sure they include references to all three days of fighting.

Thinking About the Chapter (Drawing Conclusions)   Elicit that armies have a high command that decides what to do in battles. Ask students to name the Confederate high command on the last day at Gettysburg. (*Lee, Longstreet, Pickett*) Have them describe the character of each man. Ask: In hindsight, should Pickett's Charge have been made? Since the final decision rested with Lee, what were the chances that the Rebels would follow Longstreet's advice?

CHAPTER 24 LEE THE FOX

PAGES 117-119

1 Class Period   **Homework: Student Study Guide p. 31**

Chapter Summary

Lee escaped the carnage of Gettysburg as Northern generals once again failed to press their advantage. In the West, however, Ulysses S. Grant was winning a decisive battle at the Southern stronghold of Vicksburg. In Grant, President Lincoln finally found a general willing to keep on fighting.

Key Vocabulary

deserter   siege

1. CONNECT

Have students recall moments prior to July 4, 1863, where Union generals moved too slowly. Discuss how Meade's failure to pursue Lee left the country with nearly two more years of slaughter. Note that well over half the deaths in the Civil War came after Gettysburg.

2. UNDERSTAND

1. Read the chapter. Discuss: Why was General Lee known as "the Gray Fox"? (*Lee used trickery to elude the enemy.*) How did Grant differ from McClellan and Meade in his approach to war? (*Grant had one goal: to win. He was willing to break the rules of custom and to pursue the enemy relentlessly to reach that goal.*)
2. Ask: What did Lincoln mean after the battle of Vicksburg when he said, "The father of waters flows unvexed to the sea"? (*Since the entire river was in Union hands, there would be no more conflict there.*) Why does the author discuss what happened when Moctezuma refused to surrender to Cortes? (*Moctezuma and other leaders were killed and their kingdom was destroyed. The author is asking students to compare this to the South's refusal to surrender and asking what they risk as a result.*)

3. CHECK UNDERSTANDING

Writing   Have students write from a Northern perspective a poem expressing their feelings about the fateful first week of July 1863.

Thinking About the Chapter (Analyzing)   Remind students about General Winfield Scott's original plan to defeat the South: the Anaconda plan. Ask: How well is this plan proceeding? (*Two-thirds of the plan has taken effect. The Mississippi has been taken, splitting the South. The naval blockade is increasing. All that remains to do is to capture Richmond.*)

READING NONFICTION

Analyzing Primary and Secondary Sources

Have students study the photograph of Vicksburg on page 118, read the caption, and reread the quote from Dora Miller. Ask students to write a few sentences telling whether the words or the photograph more strongly evokes the situation of the people of Vicksburg, and why.

GEOGRAPHY CONNECTIONS

Civil War Room Activity

Have students continue the Civil War Room activity as described on TG page 26. Have them locate and mark the following:

Vicksburg   32°15'N 90°52'W

READING NONFICTION

Analyzing Rhetorical Devices

Invite a volunteer to read the Gettysburg address aloud and then ask students to quote phrases they remember from the oral recitation. Discuss how language use and repetition of phrases can, as in music, help people remember words. Have partners review the text and note repetitious phrasing and contrasts Lincoln used in his speech.

HISTORY ARCHIVES

A History of US Sourcebook

#53, Abraham Lincoln, *Gettysburg Address* (1863)

MEETING INDIVIDUAL NEEDS

For below-level readers, the words of the Gettysburg Address can be difficult to understand. Fortunately, it is a short speech. Have students read the speech aloud to themselves or to a partner. Review with them parts of the speech that are still difficult, and have them practice those parts.

MORE ABOUT...

Writing the Address

There are many stories about Lincoln writing his speech at the last minute, and even on the train to Gettysburg. These stories are untrue. While Lincoln did make minor edits in the days preceding the occasion, he had been working on the address for weeks.

NOTE FROM THE AUTHOR

Thomas Jefferson wrote: "We hold these truths to be self-evident, that all men are created equal." Now listen to Lincoln's words: "Four score and seven years ago our fathers brought forth on this continent, a new nation, conceived in liberty, and dedicated to the proposition that all men are created equal...." In the Gettysburg Address, Lincoln took us back to the Declaration of Independence. Before the Civil War, the Declaration was not often seen as the central document defining America. It was Abraham Lincoln who helped make it so.

CHAPTER 25 · SPEECHES AT GETTYSBURG

PAGES 119-123

1 Class Period   Homework: Student Study Guide p. 32

Chapter Summary

Lincoln said in his Gettysburg Address, "The world will little note, nor long remember, what we say here." His two-minute speech not only changed the nature of the war, it has become one of the most important statements on liberty ever written.

Key Vocabulary

orator   score

1. CONNECT

Read these phrases to your students: "Four score and seven years ago," "government of the people, by the people, and for the people shall not perish from this earth." Ask students to identify the quotes and what speech they are from.

2. UNDERSTAND

1. Read pages 119-120. Discuss: Why did people gather at Gettysburg on November 19, 1863? (*to dedicate a national cemetery honoring Union soldiers who had fallen at Gettysburg*)
2. Discuss: Why did Lincoln accept the invitation to speak at Gettysburg? (*He wanted to address the Northern desire to end the war and let the South break off from the Union. He needed to inspire people so the dream of the founders could continue.*)
3. Read the rest of the chapter and complete Resource Page 8 (TG page 106) to take a closer look at the Gettysburg Address.

3. CHECK UNDERSTANDING

Writing Have students write a one-paragraph account of November 19, 1863, at Gettysburg as if they were Edward Everett. Have them make their account passionate and eloquent.

Thinking About the Chapter (Understanding Cause and Effect) Have students examine the image and newspaper headline on page 121. Discuss the connection between the New York draft riots and Lincoln's words at Gettysburg. (*Lincoln recognized the draft riots, in which much of the hostility was directed at blacks, as a sign that many forces in the North were still blind to the larger aims of the war. He needed to inspire people to overcome their smaller prejudices for the cause of preserving democracy.*)

CHAPTER 26
MORE BATTLES— WILL IT EVER END?
PAGES 124–130

2 Class Periods   **Homework: Student Study Guide p. 33**

Chapter Summary

The Southern strategy of wearing the North out nearly worked. Northerners were getting tired. Political forces were trying to replace Lincoln with General McClellan who offered peace if elected president in 1864. Lincoln feared he would not be able to see the nation through its terrible ordeal unless the winds of war changed in his favor. As Grant was occupying Lee in bloody combat in Virginia, two other Union generals—Sherman and Sheridan—used total war to drive the South to its knees.

1. CONNECT

Remind students of General Winfield Scott's Anaconda plan. Elicit that it was the logical plan for the North, but it was not easy to execute. Tell students that after three years, it was finally reaching fruition, but that many thousands of men would still have to die and the South would be almost destroyed before the war ended.

2. UNDERSTAND

1. Read pages 124-126. Discuss: What were Grant's plans in 1864? What was his strategy? (*His goal was to capture Richmond and Lee's army. His strategy was to wear Lee down by repeatedly attacking.*)
2. Read the rest of the chapter. Ask: What approach to fighting did Sherman and Sheridan use? (*They employed total war, in which they destroyed everything in their path to weaken the South's ability and will to fight.*) How did their successes help save the Union? (*They helped Lincoln win reelection. If McClellan had won, there was a chance that the Confederacy would remain an independent country.*)

3. CHECK UNDERSTANDING

Writing   Have students write a one- or two-paragraph synopsis of the chapter. Ask them to include a summary of Grant's and Sherman's 1864 campaigns.

Thinking About the Chapter (Making Judgments)   Divide the class in half. Then write the following statement on the chalkboard: "General William Tecumseh Sherman is a true American hero." One half of the class will be the *pro* side, the other the *con* side. Give students 5-10 minutes to review pages 127-129. Students will have to confront the use of total war in the service of a higher good—that of keeping the Union together.

GEOGRAPHY CONNECTIONS

Civil War Room Activity
Have students continue the Civil War Room activity as described on TG page 26. Have them locate and mark the following:

Sherman's march	
Sheridan's ride	
Atlanta	33°45'N 84°22'W
Savannah	32°00'N 81°00'W

ACTIVITIES/JOHNS HOPKINS TEAM LEARNING

See the Student Team Learning Activity on TG page 78.

JOHNS HOPKINS TEAM LEARNING

THE YANKEES ARE COMING!

1 CLASS PERIOD

FOCUS ACTIVITY

1. Ask students how many of them have kept a diary of things that happened to them over a period of time. Elicit that diaries are usually filled with personal reactions to events.

2. Have students contrast how a person's diary reports an event with how a secondary source such as a textbook would report the same event. Lead students to recognize that a diary gives a small, intense view of an event, whereas a textbook usually gives a wider, more thoughtful view of the event. Explain that both views are useful in understanding history.

STUDENT TEAM LEARNING ACTIVITY/ANALYZING PRIMARY AND SECONDARY SOURCES

1. Divide the class into teams of four. Have teams **Partner Read** Chapter 26, using main idea and detail charts to record the information in the chapter.

2. Distribute copies of Resource Page 9 (TG page 107). Team members should take turns reading the entries aloud to the team.

3. Have teams use **Think-Team-Share** to compare and contrast the content and effect of the primary and secondary sources.

4. Bring the class together to reinforce the learning.

Part 5 Check-Up Use Check-Up 5 (TG page 97) to assess student learning in Part 5.

ALTERNATE ASSESSMENT
Ask students to write an essay answering one of the following questions, which link the big ideas across chapters.

1. Making Connections How are the following Civil War events connected: Antietam, Emancipation Proclamation, 54th Massachusetts assault on Fort Wagner? (*Students should note that, without the victory at Antietam, Lincoln would not have been able to issue the Emancipation Proclamation; and that without the Proclamation changing the meaning of the war, African Americans would not have been able to fight for freedom.*)

2. Making Connections Have pairs of students write a conversation between Robert E. Lee and Ulysses S. Grant in which the men discuss the question, "How and why did the South eventually lose the war?"

DEBATING THE ISSUES
Use the topic below to stimulate debate.

Resolved That the North should cease fighting and pursue peace with the South in the summer of 1864. (To provoke debate, appoint several students to speak for McClellan and for people who oppose the draft. Others should represent the views of free blacks such as Frederick Douglass. Still others should speak for Abraham Lincoln and generals such as Grant. Finally, a few students might talk for the South. Encourage these students to explain why it is in the North's advantage to stop fighting.

MAKING ETHICAL JUDGMENTS
The following activity asks students to consider issues of ethics.

Suppose you are a free black. You've just heard about the Emancipation Proclamation and Union plans to use black soldiers. You have found out also that these soldiers must serve in segregated units, and that all commanders will be white. Will you sign up? Why or why not? (*Answers will vary widely. But lead students to understand the commitment of free blacks to free enslaved brothers and sisters in the South.*)

PROJECTS AND ACTIVITIES
Writing a Letter Read aloud the passage from Lincoln's letter to General McClellan cited in the margin of page 90: "Dear General, if you do not want to use the army I would like to borrow it for a few days." Then assign students to write a letter that McClellan might have sent back to Lincoln. Ask volunteers to share their letters with the class.

NOTE FROM THE AUTHOR
When a 10-year-old in a San Diego school peppered me with questions about the Civil War, I asked where he had learned so much. Seems he had read all three massive volumes of Shelby Foote's The Civil War. *I was astonished, but then I remembered that as a child I often read books that were over my head. Of course I missed much that the author was saying, but that never bothered me—I got enough to make it worthwhile. We often deny children that mind-stretching opportunity. We peg books to what we adults see as their reading level. I urge you to encourage your students to read whatever they wish and—I know this is heresy—even to skip parts that don't interest them. (I do it all the time.) The main thing is to get them to read and to think—and to find delight in both.*

USING THE RUBRICS
To assess these writing assignments, group projects, and activities, scoring rubrics have been provided at the back of this Teaching Guide. Be sure to explain the rubrics to your students.

Making Inferences

Tell students that in April 1865, African American poet Francis Watkins Harper wrote the following lines in a letter.

> *To-day a nation sits down beneath the shadow of its mournful grief. . . . Moses, the meekest man on earth, led the children of Israel over the Red Sea, but was not permitted to see them settled in [the Promised Land]. Mr. Lincoln has led [us] up through another Red Sea to the table land of triumphant victory, and God has seen fit to summon for the new era another man.*

Harper uses several biblical analogies. Request volunteers to identify and explain them. Then have students infer from this letter the fate of Lincoln. What evidence in the selection supports their inferences?

Writing a News Article Assign students to write a news article headlined "General Jackson Shot By Wild Fire." The article should be written from the perspective of a Southern reporter. Direct students to answer as many of the reporter's questions as possible: Who? What? Where? When? Why? How? Articles might also include quotes from General Lee.

Writing Eyewitness Accounts Read aloud, or distribute copies, of the following account of the battle between the *Monitor* and the *Merrimack* written by a Confederate officer:

> *The first shots of the Merrimack were directed at the [wooden ship] Minnesota. . . . But the Monitor placed herself between the Merrimack and her intended victim. From that moment the conflict became a heroic single combat between the two ironclads.*

Direct students to finish this account as if they were Confederate eyewitnesses to the battle. Remind students to keep in mind the drama that an eyewitness probably felt.

Designing a Poster Tell students that David Farragut's father, Jorge Farragut, came to the American colonies from the Spanish island of Minorca during the American Revolution. He served as a lieutenant in the South Carolina Navy and fought the British at Savannah and Charleston. Farragut spoke Spanish and remained proud of his heritage all his life. When Farragut met the queen of Spain in 1867, she remarked: "I am proud to know that your ancestors came from my kingdom." Direct students to use this background, as well as information in the text, to design a poster for Hispanic Heritage Month (September 15-October 15) in which Farragut's achievements are celebrated. If time allows, encourage students to do additional research into other Latinos who took part in the Civil War. Possible choices include Loretta Velazquez, Colonel Manuel Chaves, Lola Sanchez, Frederico Fernandez Cavada.

Composing Song Lyrics On December 31, 1862, the eve of Lincoln's historic signing of the Emancipation Proclamation, a group of contrabands composed a new spiritual. It began:

> *Go down, Abraham, away down in*
> *Dixie's land,*
> *Tell Jefferson Davis to let my people go.*

Request volunteers to compose additional lines to this spiritual. Musically talented students might set the lyrics to music.

Writing Summaries Instruct small groups of students to imagine they are military advisers assigned to keep Lincoln informed of events at Gettysburg. Have students write five telegraph messages in which they summarize the following phases of action: arrival of Confederate troops in Gettysburg; Confederate occupation of Seminary Ridge; shelling of Union troops on Cemetery Hill; Pickett's Charge; aftermath of the battle. Each

THE BIG IDEAS

On April 9, 1865, the Civil War ended in a handshake between Robert E. Lee and Ulysses S. Grant. Five days later, an assassin's bullet cut down the president who promised "malice toward none." Southern hopes for a just peace turned to ashes. Wrote one Southern editor:

> LINCOLN IS DEAD. They [the assassins] have conspired against his life, have sought and taken it, toward whom he had not one thought of hate, to who he had again and again made most gracious offers of peace and pardon....[W]hen Abraham Lincoln fell, the South lost its best and truest friend.

Part 6 tells the story of the closing conflicts of the Civil War. Defeat of the South cleared the way for Americans to continue their quest for liberty. But the tragic death of Lincoln deprived them of the compassionate leader needed to guide the nation on its unfinished journey.

INTRODUCING PART 6

SETTING GOALS
Introduce Part 6 by asking a classic "what if" question: What if Lincoln had not been assassinated? Help students understand that at a key moment of need, the country lost the one person who would have best helped it heal itself. Ask students to think about what qualities Lincoln had that would have made him effective after the war. (*compassion, respect, deep sense of the long-term need to reconnect the country*)

To set goals for Part 6, tell students that they will
- paraphrase the key idea in Lincoln's second inaugural address.
- explain the significance of taking Richmond.
- describe Lincoln's assassination and analyze reactions to his death.
- evaluate whether the gains achieved by the Civil War were worth the price.

SETTING A CONTEXT FOR READING
Thinking About the Big Ideas   Ask students to consider the hypothetical situation posed by the author on page 130: "Suppose you have a terrible fight with a friend. Suppose that friend really hurts you. What would you do when the fight is over?" Request volunteers to explain how they would resolve the conflict. Use this discussion to explore how Lincoln might plan to deal with the South once the Civil War was over. To present their theories, groups of students can draft a two-paragraph address that Lincoln might deliver upon his second inauguration. Post these addresses on the bulletin board for comparison with the selection from the actual speech reprinted on page 132.

CHAPTERS 27-31]
27 The Second Inaugural   130
28 Closing In on the End   133
29 Mr. McLean's Parlor   138
30 A Play at Ford's Theatre   143
31 After Words   147

Interpreting Pictures and Evaluating Author's Purpose
Have students skim Part 6 to find images of Abraham Lincoln.
For each, have students analyze the meaning and explain why
they think the image was selected for the book. What does it say
about Lincoln?

SETTING A CONTEXT IN SPACE AND TIME
Linking Geography and History   Refer students to the wall
map of Civil War battles suggested for Part 5, or use their Civil
War Room maps. Ask where most of the battles took place during the final months of war. (*Virginia*) Ask students to predict
what will happen next. How will the war end?

Setting a Time Frame   Read aloud the sidenote on page 130.
Ask students to identify the time period covered by Part 6.
(*March 4-April 15, 1865*) Then refer them to the Chronology on
page 153. How do the events listed for this time span prove the
author's claim that this "is an important time in American history"?

27 THE SECOND INAUGURAL
PAGES 130-132

1 Class Period   **Homework: Student Study Guide p. 34**

Chapter Summary
As the war drew to a close, Lincoln saw hope amid the destruction. He promised to "bind up the nation's wounds" so that the ideals of the Declaration of Independence could finally be realized.

Key Vocabulary
Reconstruction   malice

1. CONNECT

Have students recall that at the end of the American Revolution the new United States faced many challenges. The country was in debt, there were hard feelings between Patriots and Loyalists, other nations saw the new nation as vulnerable, and there were political divisions. Point out that sometimes the impact of war is determined by how the peace is handled.

2. UNDERSTAND

1. Read the chapter. Discuss: How had Lincoln's feelings about war changed by the time of his second inauguration? (*He saw the war as having a new purpose—as part of a God-given plan to end slavery.*) The author wants to know: What did Lincoln mean when he said it was unjust for people to be "wringing their bread from the sweat of other men's faces"? (*That people should not support themselves from the forced labor of others.*)
2. What hope did Lincoln's second inaugural address hold out to both North and South? (*It promised a just peace that would honor those who had died in the name of liberty and that would allow the North and South to come together.*)

3. CHECK UNDERSTANDING

Writing Have students complete the following writing exercise: Imagine that you are a Northern mother from Chicago, Illinois, who has lost her three sons in the war. Write a paragraph expressing your conflicting feelings when you read President Lincoln's second inaugural address in the newspaper.

Thinking About the Chapter (Evaluating) Have volunteers read aloud Lincoln's Second Inaugural Address. Ask how people from the North and South might feel about his words. Discuss the short-term irony of Lincoln's words while Northern armies were devastating the South.

MEETING INDIVIDUAL NEEDS
Pair students who are learning English with thos who are proficient to read Lincoln's Second Inaugural Address together. Have pairs paraphrase the passages of the address.

ACTIVITIES/JOHNS HOPKINS TEAM LEARNING
See the Student Team Learning Activity on TG page 88.

HISTORY ARCHIVES
A History of US Sourcebook
#55, Abraham Lincoln, *Second Inaugural Address* (1865)

Civil War Room Activity

Have students continue the Civil War Room activity as described on TG page 26. Have them locate and mark the following:

Washington D.C.   38°52'N 77°00'W

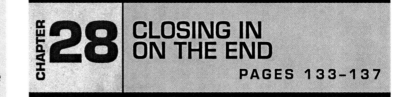

1 Class Period   **Homework: Student Study Guide p. 35**

Chapter Summary
After four years of horrible war, Grant finally captured Richmond. As Lincoln visited the fallen capital, the joy of blacks and the fear of white Southerners convinced him that the time had come to build a stronger, more democratic government.

1. CONNECT

Chapter 27 focuses on Lincoln's second inaugural, at which he urged "malice toward none." Have students predict Lincoln's behavior if he was able to visit a conquered Richmond. What could he do to lead by example?

2. UNDERSTAND

1. Read pages 133-135 up to "Of course they would fight." Discuss: How did the 13th Amendment go beyond the Emancipation Proclamation? *(It made emancipation the law of the land.)* What event showed the end of the Civil War was near? (*the fall of Richmond*) What did Lincoln, Grant, and Sherman discuss at City Point? *(how, although the war was harsh, the peace should be gentle)*
2. Read the rest of the chapter. Discuss: Why did Lincoln go to Richmond? What happened when he was there? (*He went to make a statement to the South that he was their president and always had been. He also wanted to show mercy. While he was there, former slaves surrounded him to show gratitude.*)

3. CHECK UNDERSTANDING

Writing Have students write a short essay explaining the significance of each of the following: Lincoln's meeting with Grant and Sherman, the battle of Five Forks, and Lincoln's visit to Richmond.

Thinking About the Chapter (Using Historical Imagination)
Have students imagine they are each of the following: a former slave, the child of a Confederate soldier, a Union soldier. Lead a discussion on how each person would have described Lincoln's visit to Richmond. (*Possible responses: Former slave—Lincoln as liberator and friend; Confederate child—as a person who might punish your father; Union soldier—as a symbol of the ideals for which the North fought.*)

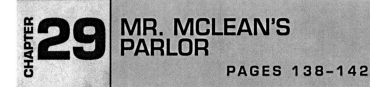

1 Class Period   Homework: Student Study Guide p. 36

Key Vocabulary
prohibit

Chapter Summary
Meeting in the parlor of Wilmer McLean's home, Grant and Lee agreed on terms of surrender. Grant's terms were kind and began the process of putting the country back together. Meanwhile, Lincoln and Congress moved ahead with plans to pass the 13th Amendment, ending slavery in the United States.

1. CONNECT

Tell students that one of the great ironies of history is that the Civil War began and ended in the "same place"—Wilmer McLean's farm.

2. UNDERSTAND

1. Read pages 138-139 up to "On April 9, 1865...." Discuss: Who was Wilmer McLean? (*He was an average American who happened to live in Manassas at the beginning of the war and Appomattox at the end of the war. His home figured directly in both events.*)

2. Read the rest of the chapter. Ask: What were the provisions of the 13th, 14th, and 15th Amendments? (*The 13th abolished slavery; the 14th gave equal protection to all Americans; the 15th said all citizens have the right to vote, although it did not extend the franchise to women.*)

3. What were the terms of surrender? (*He allowed soldiers to go home if they agreed to not fight again; he did not press charges of treason; he took the soldiers' guns, but allowed them to keep their horses; he allowed officers to keep their sidearms.*) What is the significance of Ely Parker's statement, "We are all Americans"? (*The country was reunited. Although a terrible war had been fought over sectional differences, the country was still based on the idea that "all men are created equal."*)

3. CHECK UNDERSTANDING

Writing   Have students write a short paragraph supporting the following statement: "The finest hour for Generals Grant and Lee was their meeting at Appomattox."

Thinking About the Chapter (Visualizing the Past)   Use the painting on page 140 to re-enact the scene in the McLeans' parlor. Instruct students to try to capture the mood and personality of the occasion.

READING NONFICTION
Analyzing Word Choice
Discuss that the author uses figurative language to make historical information come alive. Ask: What does the author mean by "McLean had magnets in his blood?" (*He seemed to attract historic events.*) Have students find and explain other figurative language used in the chapter.

GEOGRAPHY CONNECTIONS
Civil War Room Activity
Have students continue the Civil War Room activity as described on TG page 26. Have them locate and mark the following:

Appomattox   37°15'N 78°45'W

HISTORY ARCHIVES
A History of US Sourcebook
1. #56, Ulysses S. Grant and Robert E. Lee, *Letters Setting Terms of Lee's Surrender at Appomattox* (1865)
2. #57, Robert E. Lee, *Farewell to His Army*, (1865)

LINKING DISCIPLINES

History/Poetry

Have students complete Resource Page 10 (TG page 114) to analyze Walt Whitman's eulogy to Lincoln, "O Captain! My Captain!" Nothing captures the feeling of the nation after Lincoln was lost like Whitman's poem. You may wish to have volunteers read the poem aloud to the class, or have students read to partners.

NOTE FROM THE AUTHOR

Senator Henry Clay was a model of what Abraham Lincoln believed a statesman should be. When Clay died, Lincoln delivered a eulogy; in lauding Clay, he spoke of his vision of an ideal politician:

> *Mr. Clay's eloquence did not consist…of [an]…elegant arrangement of words and sentences…but rather of that deeply earnest and impassioned tone and manner, which can proceed only from great sincerity and a thorough conviction in the speaker of the justice and importance of his cause.…He never spoke merely to be heard.…*
>
> *Mr. Clay's predominant sentiment, from first to last, was a deep devotion to the cause of human liberty, a strong sympathy with the oppressed everywhere, and an ardent wish for their elevation. With him this was a primary and all-controlling passion.…He loved his country partly because it was his own country, but mostly because it was a free country; and he burned with a zeal for its advancement, prosperity and glory, because he saw in such, the advancement, prosperity, and glory of human liberty, human rights, and human nature. He desired the prosperity of his countrymen partly because they were his countrymen, but chiefly to show to the world that free men could be prosperous.*

Have your students read those words and substitute Lincoln's name for Clay's. Did Lincoln achieve his vision of political greatness? How would your students describe the ideal statesman?

30 A PLAY AT FORD'S THEATRE

CHAPTER

PAGES 143-146

1 Class Period   **Homework: Student Study Guide p. 37**

Chapter Summary

Lincoln was in a good mood on April 14, 1865. He was making plans for reconstructing the Union with his cabinet. However, the bullet that claimed Lincoln's life that night changed the course of Reconstruction. The voice of moderation and forgiveness at the head of government was removed.

Key Vocabulary

Reconstruction

1. CONNECT

This chapter is about an assassination, the death of a great person. Ask students to recall other leaders who have been killed for their beliefs. (*John Kennedy, Martin Luther King, Jr., Malcolm X, religious leaders*) Then ask students if they think these people knew there were risks in taking a leadership role. Does this lead students to have more respect for current leaders?

2. UNDERSTAND

1. Read the chapter. Discuss: What did Lincoln and his cabinet discuss in their meeting on the day Lincoln was shot? (*how best to rebuild the nation*)
2. Discuss: Who killed Lincoln? How? What happened to him? (*John Wilkes Booth, a disgruntled Southern actor, shot Lincoln while he was attending a play at Ford's Theatre. He was captured and killed several days later.*)
3. What did Elizabeth Keckley mean when she called Lincoln "the Moses of my people"? (*He was the person who helped lead slaves out of bondage, as Moses led the Hebrews out of bondage.*)

3. CHECK UNDERSTANDING

Writing Have students reread the quotes about Lincoln's passing on page 146, including Keckley's writing. Then ask students to place themselves in 1865 and write a paragraph about Lincoln's death expressing their own feelings.

Thinking About the Chapter (Analyzing) Engage the class in a discussion using the following prompt: "If John Wilkes Booth really loved the South, the last person he would want to see dead would be Abraham Lincoln." Have students use the details about Lincoln from the chapter to support this statement.

CHAPTER

31 AFTER WORDS

PAGES 147–149

1 Class Period   **Homework: Student Study Guide p. 38**

Chapter Summary
The Civil War proved the strength of the American vision of a republic. New amendments ended the evils of slavery. But the task of wiping out the inequalities born of racism still lay ahead.

Key Vocabulary
scalawag

1. CONNECT

Ask students to think back over their study of the Civil War. Ask: What have they found the most interesting? In the end, do they feel that forcing the South to rejoin the Union was worth the cost? Explain that the author states her opinion in the final chapter.

2. UNDERSTAND

1. Read the chapter. What did George Pickett mean when he said "the South has lost her best friend and protector." (*No other politician would be strong enough to subdue the desire for revenge among many Northerners.*)
2. If Lincoln could speak to Americans today, what might he say the Civil War had accomplished? (*Answers will vary, but students should mention such things as preservation of the Union, end of slavery, and protection of liberty through the 13th, 14th, and 15th Amendments.*)

3. CHECK UNDERSTANDING

Writing   Have students write a paragraph evaluating whether the gains of the Civil War were worth the costs.

Thinking About the Chapter (Analyzing)   The author mentions several achievements of the war, two of which she calls "remarkable." Have students discuss these results—the nation holding together, the republic surviving, no guerrilla war after the war ended, a rebirth of freedom—and how they benefit us as a nation today.

READING NONFICTION
Analyzing Rhetorical Devices
Ask students to find the phrasing at the beginning of the chapter that is echoed at the end. (*"Oh, murder most foul! Oh, woe! Oh, tragedy!"* and at the end, *"Oh tragedy."*) Explain that these phrases are taken from one of William Shakespeare's plays. Discuss how these phrases emphasize the authors view of events, as well as the feelings of the nation.

Have students read the plea the author makes in the next-to-last paragraph, "When you are old enough to vote...." Have students discuss why she addresses readers directly rather than expressing her thoughts another way. Why is this statement especially effective coming at the end of this book?

JOHNS HOPKINS TEAM LEARNING

LINCOLN'S SECOND INAUGURAL ADDRESS

1 EXTENDED CLASS PERIOD

FOCUS ACTIVITY

1. Read the following list of "One Man's Failures," a synopsis of Lincoln's life, and have students guess who is being described:

> *Born into a struggling farm family. At age 8, mother died. Had less than one year of school. Lost his job in 1832. Defeated for state legislature in 1832. Failed in business in 1833. Sweetheart died in 1835. Had serious depression in 1836. Defeated for nomination for Congress in 1843. Rejected for land officer in 1849. Defeated for U.S. Senate in 1854. Defeated for nomination for Vice President in 1856. Defeated for U.S. Senate in 1858. Elected President in 1860.*

2. Discuss the character traits (perseverance, intelligence, honesty, faith, integrity, etc.) that allowed Lincoln to rise above his failures, educate himself, and eventually become a great leader.

STUDENT TEAM LEARNING ACTIVITY/READING AND ANALYZING A PRIMARY SOURCE

1. Organize the class into six teams. Copy and distribute Lincoln's Second Inaugural Address, found in *A History of US Sourcebook.*

2. Assign each team one section of the address. (You may decide how to divide the long central section of the speech.) Have one member from each team read aloud their team's excerpt to the class.

3. Have each team paraphrase their passage. Make sure students understand that they are to rewrite the passage using their own words.

4. Team members should write down the main idea of their passage in their own words. They should also use the textbook and the *Sourcebook* to try to ascertain other sources that contained these ideas. The sources can be other writings or speeches by Lincoln or other historical U.S. documents, such as the Declaration of Independence.

5. Circulate and Monitor Assist students with reading, make sure they are on task, and help resolve any difficulties.

6. Using **Numbered Heads**, have teams read their passages and their paraphrased versions, and report on any connections to other sources that they found.

ASSESSMENT

Part 6 Check-Up   Use Check-Up 6 (TG page 98) to assess student learning in Part 6.

ALTERNATE ASSESSMENT
Ask students to write an essay answering the following question, which links the big ideas across the chapters.

Making Connections   At the end of the Civil War, one young Southern woman wrote: "The most terrible part of the war is still to come." Discuss several of the horrors Southerners had to go through during the war. Then explain why you think Southerners felt the conflict had not ended for them. (*Help students synthesize some of the difficulties faced by the South—total war, burning of their major cities, terrible sieges of Vicksburg and Petersburg, etc. Then lead students to understand that Southerners were well aware that reconstructing the Union would involve great hardships as well.*)

ASSESSING PART 6

DEBATING THE ISSUES
The topic below can be used to stimulate debate.

Resolved   That the South and its leaders should be punished for treason. (Encourage *pro* students to focus on the act of secession, the defense of slavery, and so on. *Con* students should represent views of Lincoln. To stir up debate even more, you might appoint a few students to represent Southerners such as Lee. You also might note that the punishment for treason can be death.)

MAKING ETHICAL JUDGMENTS
The following activity asks students to consider issues of ethics.

Imagine you are an African American at the end of the Civil War. Sherman's troops have burned the plantation where you have spent your life. You have no money and no job. Your former owner, a Confederate officer, returns home from Appomattox. He asks you to stay on the plantation to work. Will you stay? Or will you leave to test your new freedom? Remember the rest of the South is in shambles as well and most of your family is too old or too young to travel. (*Answers will vary, but students should understand the double bind faced by the millions of African Americans seeking to build new lives. Help students assess the responsibilities of the federal government in helping African Americans throughout the South.*)

PROJECTS AND ACTIVITIES
Writing a News Article   Distribute copies of the following incomplete news article. Tell students it is based on an actual account from a reporter for the *Boston Journal*.

SUMMARIZING PART 6

NOTE FROM THE AUTHOR

How about testing? How will children do if they study these books? The old books focus on narrow, easy-to-memorize test questions. When children meet new questions, they are lost. This program challenges children to question, to develop their minds, to do research and writing, to think for themselves—as well as to learn specifics about the past. That is exactly what the SAT and the new tests look for.

USING THE RUBRICS

To assess these writing assignments, group projects, and activities, scoring rubrics have been provided at the back of this Teaching Guide. Be sure to explain the rubrics to your students.

Making Predictions

Tell students that in 1882, Frederick Douglass made the following assessment of the Civil War:

> *Though slavery was abolished, the wrongs of my people were not ended. Though they were not slaves, they were not yet quite free. No man can be truly free whose liberty is dependent upon the thought, feeling, and action of others, and who has himself no means in his own hands for guarding, protecting, defending, and maintaining that liberty.*

After thinking about this quote, what can students infer about the course of Reconstruction?

Richmond, VA.—April 4, 1865. It was the man of the people among the people. It was the great deliverer meeting the delivered.…He was so tall, so conspicuous.

Ask students to use information in the text to complete the story. Explain that the reporter has written the "hook" to grab the reader's attention. It's their job to supply the who, what, when, where, how, and why of the story.

Doing Research   Review the story of Ely Parker. Then have students research how the Civil War touched other Native Americans. More advanced students might investigate the stories in *The Civil War in the American West*, by Alvin M. Josephy, Jr. Other students can read "An Indian Civil War" in *Black Indians*, by William Loren Katz. Call on students to present their findings in short oral reports.

Putting It in Your Own Words   Make copies of the full text of the 13th, 14th, and 15th Amendments. Distribute these to groups of students, and assign them to rewrite the amendments in everyday language. (You might allow students who are learning English to work in their primary language, translating it into English when they are done.)

Creating a Brochure   Challenge students to design a brochure that the Virginia Office of Tourism might distribute to people visiting Appomattox Courthouse. The brochure should include a guided tour of the sites on the map on pages 140-141.

Writing Poetry   At the conclusion of the Civil War, Frances Ellen Watkins Harper lifted her pen to celebrate the end of slavery. Copy the following opening verse on the chalkboard. Assign students to complete the poem, expressing the hopes of African Americans at the time.

> *God bless our native land,*
> *Land of the newly free,*
> *OH may she ever stand*
> *For truth and liberty.*

Updating History   Tell students that when Lincoln first entered Congress, he wrote the following autobiographical entry in the Congressional Directory:

> *Born February 12, 1809 in Hardin County, Kentucky. Education, defective. Profession, lawyer. Have been a captain of volunteers in the Black Hawk War. Postmaster in a very small office. Four times a member of the Illinois Legislature and a member of the Lower House of Congress.*

Ask students to imagine that the Congressional historian has asked Lincoln to update this account on April 12, 1865. What would Lincoln write?

Use the following questions to help students pull together some of the major concepts and themes covered in this book. Note: You may want to assign these as essay questions for assessment.

1. In 1860, poet James Russell Lowell wrote: "The crime of [Northern States] is the census of 1860. Their increase in numbers, wealth, and power is an...aggression. It would not be enough to please the Southern States that we should stop asking them to abolish slavery....Our very thoughts are a menace." Lowell is saying that the size and power of the North were a threat to the South and by themselves would have brought about war. Do you agree with Lowell? Would war have resulted even if the North stopped pressing for abolition? Why or why not? (*Answers will vary, but you might point out that Lincoln made it clear that Union was his first goal, not abolition. Encourage students to find evidence that supports Lowell's remarks in Prefaces I and II.*)

2. A favorite question among historians is: Do individuals shape history or are individuals shaped by the times in which they live? Pick one of the following people: Abraham Lincoln, Harriet Beecher Stowe, Harriet Tubman, or John Brown. Decide whether they would have had an equal impact upon history had they lived in another era, say the early 1800s or even today. Explain the reasons for your opinion. (*Answers will vary. To elicit discussion, have students consider how history might have differed if these individuals had not lived. Would the Civil War have happened nonetheless?*)

3. What advantages and disadvantages did the Union and Confederacy each possess at the start of the Civil War? If you had been a foreign observer, what prediction might you have made about the outcome of the war? (*Answers will vary, but remind students to avoid hindsight. Most people, including Lincoln, were unsure of the course of the war.*)

4. Susie Kind Taylor, a former slave, served as a Union nurse. Said Taylor to one reporter: "What a wonderful revolution!" Why might Taylor have called the Civil War a revolution? (*Students should emphasize that for blacks the war represented a complete overthrow of the system that imprisoned them. As a tip, you might repeat another remark by Taylor: "We ask to be citizens of these United States...so that the stars and stripes will no longer be polluted [by slavery].*)

5. Many people consider the Preamble to the Declaration of Independence and the Gettysburg Address as the two greatest statements of American liberty. What ideals do these two documents share? (*Both documents uphold the ideals of liberty and equality. The Gettysburg Address reaffirms government by consent of the people.*)

6. By 1865, many Northerners had come to believe that abolition of slavery was the chief aim of the war. Do you think Lin-

SYNTHESIZING THE BIG IDEAS IN BOOK SIX

NOTE FROM THE AUTHOR

I see the central theme of all my books as the American quest for those ideals so eloquently articulated in the Declaration of Independence. The goal of equality for all—which is a fairness quest.

If you charted that quest, you would see peaks and valleys. As a nation, we have often been unfair; our government has been repressive; many Americans are unable to fulfill their dreams. But despite all that, the chart flows upward. We have incredible goals; the journey, which continues, is not easy.

coln agreed? If so, why? If not, what did he feel was the chief aim of the war? (*Answers will vary. Students who agree may cite Lincoln's support of the 13th Amendment. Students who disagree might mention Lincoln's vision of the war as a test of free, democratic government.*)

7. Lincoln promised Americans "a new birth of freedom." What tools did the Civil War give them to build this new vision of America? (*Students should mention provisions in the 13th, 14th, and 15th Amendments.*)

CHECK-UP 1

Answering the following questions will help you understand and remember what you have read in the Prefaces and Chapters 1-2. Write your answers on a separate sheet of paper.

1. Imagine you are traveling on the "Road to Civil War." Along the way, you meet each of the following figures. Identify each person. Then explain how his actions relate to the growing conflict. (Note: The road stretches far back in time.)
   a. Andrew Jackson
   b. John Calhoun
   c. Patrick Henry
   d. Ralph Waldo Emerson
   e. P. G. T. Beauregard
   f. T. J. "Stonewall" Jackson

2. Now review some of the sites that you have passed during your journey along the "Road to Civil War." Write brief historical markers to guide other travelers.
   a. Brown's Indian Queen Hotel
   b. Jamestown
   c. Fort Sumter
   d. Manassas (Bull Run)
   e. Richmond, Virginia

3. During your trip, you've heard some special terms. Define each of the following terms, and explain how it relates to the growing crisis.
   a. federal Union
   b. peculiar institution
   c. states' rights
   d. abolitionists
   e. Rebels
   f. Federals
   g. secede
   h. Rebel yell

4. Send a postcard to one of your friends in the present. Describe some aspect of your journey that mentions at least two of the people, places, or terms from questions 1-3.

5. The author says that a "conflict of ideas would create the worst war in all our history." What ideas were in conflict?

6. What was the connection between slavery and the South's economy?

7. Some Southerners referred to the Civil War as the Second War for Independence. How might President Lincoln have responded to that description? Explain.

8. Write two headlines describing the capture of Fort Sumter—one for a newspaper in Charleston and the other for a newspaper in Boston. How do the two headlines differ?

9. Suppose you are a member of Congress after the First Battle of Manassas (Bull Run). What will you report about the Union's chances for winning the war? Why?

10. **Thinking About the Big Ideas** In 1913, historian James Ford Rhodes wrote: "Of the American Civil War it may safely be asserted that there was a single cause, slavery." Do you agree or disagree? Explain.

CHECK-UP 2

Answering the following questions will help you understand and remember what you have read in Chapters 3-10. Write your answers on a separate sheet of paper.

1. Each person listed below played a key role in the events described in Chapters 3-10. Identify each person and tell what he or she did to increase the conflict between North and South.
   a. Harriet Beecher Stowe
   b. Harriet Tubman
   c. Abraham Lincoln
   d. Jefferson Davis
   e. John Brown

2. Suppose you were a Lincoln fan who wanted to find out more about your hero. Why might you want to visit each of the following sites?
   a. Kentucky
   b. Little Pigeon Creek, Indiana
   c. New Salem, Illinois
   d. Springfield, Illinois
   e. Freeport, Illinois

3. Define each of the following terms. Then explain how each term is related to the struggle to win liberty for enslaved people.
   a. Underground Railroad
   b. conductors
   c. popular sovereignty
   d. Fugitive Slave Law
   e. abolitionists

4. Write a dialogue between Harriet Beecher Stowe and Abraham Lincoln in which they describe their attitudes toward slavery and slaveholders.

5. John Brown declared, "Slavery is a state of war." After meeting Harriet Tubman, he tried to recruit her for service in that war. "General Tubman," remarked Brown, "could command an army as successfully as she has led her parties of fugitives." Do you think Brown was correct in his assessment of Tubman? Why or why not? What do you think Tubman thought of Brown?

6. Put yourself in the shoes of Abraham Lincoln and Jefferson Davis. Write the first paragraph of a speech that each might have given in 1861, describing his beliefs and goals.

7. Imagine that you are a newspaper editor in 1858. Assign a short article about the Lincoln-Douglass debates to one of your reporters. Outline for the reporter the main points of the debates.

8. History is full of "what ifs." For example: what if the Virginia Assembly had voted to free enslaved people in 1831, instead of defeating the proposal by two votes? Do you think the Civil War would have taken place? Why or why not?

9. Today many African Americans consider John Brown a hero. Explain why.

10. **Thinking About the Big Ideas**   In 1860, the conflict over liberty for enslaved people reached a crisis. Do you think that President-elect Lincoln had any alternative to war? Explain.

CHECK-UP 3

Answering the following questions will help you understand and remember what you have read in Chapters 11-14. Write your answers on a separate sheet of paper.

1. Imagine you are a playwright. You want to write a drama about the Civil War entitled *The Year the Marching Began*. Identify each of the following key characters. Then describe the role you would assign to each.
    a. Abraham Lincoln
    b. Jefferson Davis
    c. Winfield Scott
    d. George McClellan
    e. Ulysses S. Grant
    f. Rose O'Neal Greenhow
    g. J. E. B. Stuart
    h. Stonewall Jackson
    i. Robert E. Lee

2. In creating your drama, why might you set scenes in each of the following locations?
    a. Richmond
    b. West Point
    c. border states
    d. Fort Sumter

3. Define the following terms. How you might use each one in your play?
    a. border states
    b. inaugural address
    c. secede
    d. blockade
    e. Anaconda Plan
    f. Confederation

4. Lincoln horrified some people when he included the following remark in his first inaugural address: "I have no purpose directly or indirectly to interfere with the institution of slavery where it exists." Why did he say that? Think back to Lincoln's early career. Was this view inconsistent with statements during the Lincoln-Douglass debates? Explain.

5. What was the Anaconda Plan? Describe how it was supposed to work and tell whether you think it was a good plan.

6. Imagine that you are Abraham Lincoln. Write a letter to General Scott telling him why you believe that General Grant will help the Union cause.

7. Robert E. Lee said, "Secession is nothing but revolution." Why then did he join the Confederacy?

8. Pretend you are a political observer in London. Describe the situation in the "States." Recommend actions you think the British government should take.

9. **Thinking About the Big Ideas**   Why would believers in states' rights want a confederation rather than a strong central government? What liberties do members of a confederation have? What conflicts are likely?

10. **Thinking About the Big Ideas**   Once the North and South picked up arms, do you think it would have been possible to end the war without settling the issue of liberty for enslaved people? Why or why not?

CHECK-UP 4

Answering the following questions will help you understand and remember what you have read in Chapters 15-17. Write your answers on a separate sheet of paper.

1. Each person listed below played a key role in events described in Chapters 15-17. Tell who each person was. Then describe the connection between the two people in each pair.
    a. J. E. B. Stuart, Philip St. George Cooke
    b. Winfield Scott Hancock, Lewis Armistead
    c. Christian Sharps, Richard Gatling
    d. Willie Lincoln, Abraham Lincoln

2. New inventions changed the geography of war. How did these inventions affect the way battles were fought on the land?
    a. new kinds of guns
    b. railroad
    c. telegraph

3. Define each of these terms. Then use each of these terms to write a description of a young soldier's life.
    a. conscription (draft)
    b. one old cat
    c. shinny
    d. sloosh
    e. breech-loading
    f. Sharps rifle
    g. artillery
    h. "Taps"

4. List some of the freedoms that we enjoy today. Then note which of these freedoms were expanded or strengthened by the Civil War.

5. Pretend you are a military historian at West Point. Prepare a short lecture that you will give to your students on how the Civil War changed the strategy and conduct of war.

6. Historian Shelby Foote says: "It was impossible to fight [the Civil War] without conscription." What factors might account for the need to start a draft in both the North and the South?

7. "We had enlisted to put down the rebellion," said one Union soldier, "and had no patience with the red-tape tomfoolery of the regular service." What does this quote tell you about the character of the soldiers who fought in the Civil War? Why might these soldiers fight differently than mercenaries, or soldiers who hire themselves out for battle?

8. In what ways was Willie Lincoln a casualty of the war?

9. What did Lincoln's private sorrows reveal about the personal costs of being president of the United States?

10. **Thinking About the Big Ideas**   The nation paid a huge price for the Civil War. Today, how do we benefit from the sacrifices of the war?

CHECK-UP 5

Answering the following questions will help you understand and remember what you have read in Chapters 18-26. Write your answers on a separate sheet of paper.

1. Each person or group listed below played a key role in events described in Chapters 18-26. Identify each person or group, and tell what each did to shape the conduct and/or outcome of the Civil War.
   a. George McClellan
   b. David Glasgow Farragut
   c. Clara Barton
   d. Massachusetts 54th
   e. George Pickett
   f. Ulysses S. Grant
   g. William Tecumseh Sherman
   h. Philip Sheridan

2. If you were drawing a map of the Civil War, why would you show the following places on your map? How was each location important to the war?
   a. Potomac River
   b. Virginia Peninsula
   c. Hampton Roads
   d. Antietam Creek
   e. Fort Wagner, South Carolina
   f. Fredericksburg, Virginia
   g. Vicksburg, Mississippi
   h. Gettysburg, Pennsylvania

3. Define each of these terms. Then explain its significance to the events of the time.
   a. hulks
   b. Emancipation Proclamation
   c. contrabands
   d. hardtack
   e. total war
   f. deserters

4. Suppose you are Abraham Lincoln. You've just turned over command of the Union armies to Ulysses S. Grant. What instructions will you give Grant?

5. Suppose you are Robert E. Lee. What eulogy will you give at the funeral of Stonewall Jackson? What words of encouragement will you give to troops mourning his loss?

6. Enslaved blacks celebrated word of the Emancipation Proclamation with a song entitled "Sixty-Three Is the Jubilee." Compose some lyrics for this song in which you express the way in which those who had been enslaved now viewed the war.

7. What strategies did the North and South each use to win the Civil War?

8. Imagine that Thomas Jefferson has returned to life. He has just read a copy of Lincoln's Gettysburg Address. How do you think the author of the Declaration of Independence might react to the speech? Explain.

9. Summarize the status of the nation at the time of Lincoln's reelection in 1864. What do you think were some of the most pressing issues?

10. **Thinking About the Big Ideas** Lincoln believed that the Emancipation Proclamation turned the conflict into a revolution. Explain reasons for this opinion. Then note whether or not you agree.

CHECK-UP 6

Answering the following questions will help you understand and remember what you have read in Chapters 27-31. Write your answers on a separate sheet of paper.

1. Imagine you are one of the key figures listed below. You want to make sure that future generations remember your role in history. For each individual, complete the following autobiographical statement: "I am important to the growth of liberty in the United States because_____."
   a. Abraham Lincoln
   b. Ulysses S. Grant
   c. Ely Parker
   d. Henry Ward Beecher
   e. Dr. John Swett Rock
   f. Salmon P. Chase

2. Imagine you are a state historian for Virginia. You have been asked to write a short book entitled *The Last Month of the Civil War: It All Happened Here.* Why would you include the following sites in your account?
   a. Petersburg
   b. City Point
   c. Richmond
   d. Appomattox Courthouse
   e. Surrender Triangle

3. Define each of the following terms. Then explain how all four terms are linked.
   a. Reconstruction
   b. 13th Amendment
   c. 14th Amendment
   d. 15th Amendment

4. Suppose you live in Charleston, South Carolina, in the 1860s. You've just read a copy of Lincoln's Second Inaugural Address. How might you respond? Why?

5. When Lincoln visited Richmond, he sat in Jefferson Davis's chair. A Union commander named James Barnes observed: "There was no triumph in his gesture or attitude. He lay back in the chair like a tired man whose nerves had carried him beyond his strength." Write a short piece in which you try to capture Lincoln's private thoughts at this moment.

6. The author says the terms of surrender offered by Grant were "kinder than anyone had expected." What were the terms? What does Joy Hakim mean?

7. List some character traits of Lincoln at the end of the war. Considering these traits, how do you think Lincoln might have defined Reconstruction?

8. Write an obituary for Lincoln that might have run in an African American newspaper at the time.

9. Consider this "what if": What if Lincoln had lived longer? Do you think history would still hold him in the same high esteem? Why or why not?

10. **Thinking About the Big Ideas**   Lincoln said: "Let us therefore study the incidents of this [war], as philosophy to learn wisdom from, and none of them as wrongs to be revenged." What wisdom do you think the Civil War taught Americans about liberty?

RESOURCE PAGE 1

Civil War Overview Map

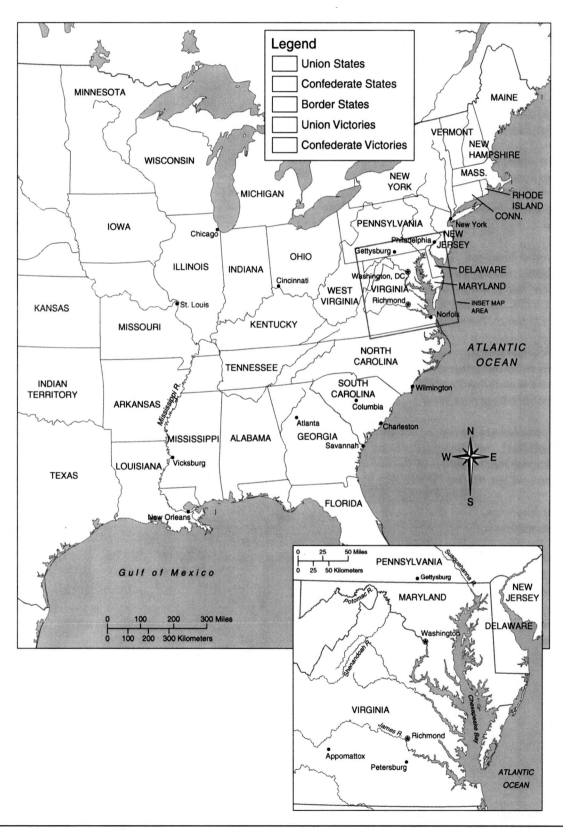

RESOURCE PAGE 2

Why They Fought

Directions: Read these quotations from Civil War soldiers. Then follow your teacher's instructions.

UNION SOLDIERS

[The United States is] the beacon light of liberty and freedom to the human race.—Sgt. Samuel McIlvaine, Indiana

Our fathers in coldest winter, half clad marked the road they trod with crimson streams from their bleeding feet that we might enjoy the blessings of a free government. Our business here [is] to lay down our lives if need be for our country's cause.—Officer Leander Stem, Ohio

Sick as I am of this war & bloodshed…I want to be at home with my dear wife & children…this war is a crusade for the good of man-kind.…I [cannot] bear to think of what my children would be if we were to permit this…conspiracy to destroy this country.—Alfred Lacey Hough, Pennsylvania

We can return to our homes with the proud satisfaction that it has been our privilege to live and take part in the struggle that has decided for all time to come that Republics are not a failure.—Col. Robert McAllister, New Jersey

There will never be peace between the two sections until slavery is so completely scotched [that]…we can see plainly in the future free labour…I think myself the Southerners are fighting against fate or human progress.—Capt. Percival Drayton, U.S. Navy

[I am defending] my Mother and Home and Country.—Pvt. Samuel Cormany, Pennsylvania

I fight…for the constitution & law. Admit the right of the seceding states to break up the Union at pleasure…& how long…before the new confederacies…shall be resolved into still smaller fragments & the continent become a vast theater of civil war.…Better settle it at whatever cost & settle it forever.—Pvt. Samuel Evans, Ohio

CONFEDERATE SOLDIERS

Fighting for the same principles which fired the hearts of our ancestors in the revolutionary struggle the South will ultimately win the war.—Cpl. Edmund Patterson, Alabama

After Lincoln's proclamation [Emancipation Proclamation] any man that would not fight to the last ought to be hung.…—Capt. John Welsh, Virginia

If I fall, let me fall, for I will fall in a good cause, for if I can not get Liberty, I prefer death.—Pvt. S. J. McLeroy, Georgia

Sink or swim, survive or perish. I will fight in defense of my country.—William E. Coleman, Kentucky

The Yankees are sacrificing their lives for nothing; we ours for home, country, and all that is dear and sacred.—Lt. Hannibal Paine, Tennessee

I am sick of war.…[Nevertheless]…were the contest just commenced I would willingly undergo it again for the sake of…our country's independence [so I can]…point with pride your children to their father as one who fought for their liberty & freedom.—Surgeon Edward W. Cade, Texas

This country without slave labor would be completely worthless.…If the negroes are freed the country is not worth fighting for…We can only live & exist by that species of labor: and hence I am willing to continue to fight to the last.—Lt. William L. Nugent, Mississippi

© OXFORD UNIVERSITY PRESS

RESOURCE PAGE 3

Uncle Tom's Cabin

Directions: Read the following excerpt from Harriet Beecher Stowe's book *Uncle Tom's Cabin*. The action involves Simon Legree, the owner of the plantation, and Tom, the enslaved hero. Then answer the questions below.

> "And now," said Legree, "come here, you Tom. You see, I told ye I didn't buy ye jest for the common work. I mean to promote ye, and make a driver of ye; and tonight ye may jest as well begin to get yer hand in. Now, ye jest take this yer gal and flog her; ye've seen enough on't to know how."
>
> "I beg mas'r's pardon," said Tom; "hopes mas'r won't set me at that. It's what I ain't used to—never did—and can't do, no way possible."
>
> "Ye'll larn a pretty smart chance of things ye never did know before I've done with ye!" said Legree, taking up a cowhide and striking Tom a heavy blow across the cheek, and following up the infliction with a shower of blows.
>
> "There!" he said, as he stopped to rest, "now will ye tell me ye can't do it?"
>
> "Yes, mas'r," said Tom, putting up his hand to wipe the blood that trickled down his face. "I'm willin' to work night and day, and work while there's life and breath in me; but this yer thing I can't feel it right to do; and mas'r, I never shall do it—never!"
>
> Tom had a remarkably smooth, soft voice, and an habitually respectful manner, that had given Legree an idea that he would be cowardly and easily subdued....
>
> Legree looked stupefied and confounded; but at last burst forth.
>
> "What! Ye blasted black beast! Tell me ye don't think it right to do what I tell ye? What have any of you cussed cattle to do with thinking what's right? I'll put a stop to it. Why, what do ye think ye are?...So you pretend it's wrong to flog the gal?"
>
> "I think so, mas'r," said Tom.... "Mas'r, if you mean to kill me, kill me; but as to my raising my hand agin anyone here I never shall—I'll die first!..."
>
> "Well, here's a pious dog at last let down among us sinners!—a saint, a gentlemen and no less, to talk of us sinners about our sins! Powerful holy critter he must be! Here, you rascal, you make believe to be so pious—didn't you never hear out of yer Bible, 'Servants, obey your masters'? An't I your master? Didn't I pay down twelve hundred dollars cash for all there is in your old cussed black shell? An't yer mine, now, body and soul?" he said, giving Tom a violent kick with his heavy boot....
>
> "No, no, no! My soul an't yours, mas'r! You haven't bought it—ye can't buy it! It's been bought and paid for by One that's able to keep it. No matter, no matter; you can't harm me!

1. What is Legree ordering Tom to do? Why won't Tom do it?

_____

_____

2. How does Legree react to Tom's refusal to do as he is ordered?

_____

3. What can you tell about Tom's character?

_____

4. Why do you think *Uncle Tom's Cabin* created outrage in the North against slavery?

_____

5. Why do you think Southern slave owners were so outraged at *Uncle Tom's Cabin*?

_____

RESOURCE PAGE 4

A House Divided—The Election of 1860

Directions: Use the information in the chart to color the states on the map, showing which candidate won the electoral votes of each state. Complete the map key. Then answer the questions below.

Electoral Votes, 1860

Party	Candidate	States Won	Votes
Republican	Lincoln	OR, CA, MN, IA, WI, IL, MI, IN, OH, PA, NY, VT, CT, RI, MA, NH, ME, NJ (split with Douglas)	180
Southern Democrat	Breckenridge	TX, LA, AR, MD, DE, MS, AL, GA, FL, SC, NC	72
Constitutional Union	Bell	TN, VA, KY	39
Northern Democrat	Douglas	MO, NJ (split with Lincoln)	12

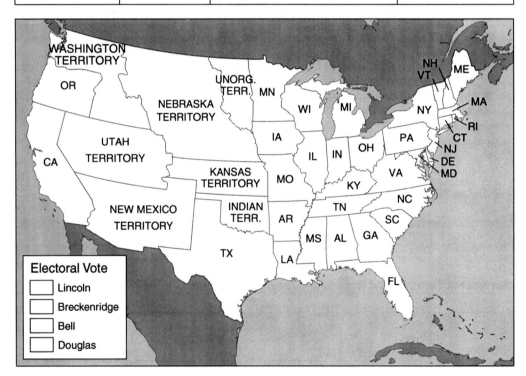

Electoral Vote
- [ ] Lincoln
- [ ] Breckenridge
- [ ] Bell
- [ ] Douglas

1. How does the map reveal the deep divisions within the country? _____

_____

2. Why might Southerners see this map as proof that the North was threatening their way of life? _____

_____

RESOURCE PAGE 5

North and South: Statistical Comparisons, 1860

Directions: Use the information in the graphs to answer the questions that follow.

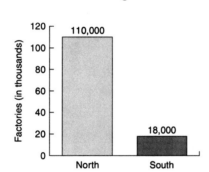

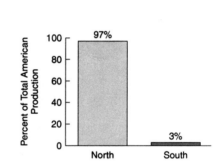

1. What was the difference in free population between the North and South in 1860?

_____

2. Of these categories, in which did the North have the greatest advantage?

_____

3. Which of these categories do you think would have the greatest effect on the war?

_____

4. Despite the overwhelming Northern economic advantages, Southerners were generally optimistic about their chances of achieving their war goals. Explain why.

_____

_____

RESOURCE PAGE 6

North and South: Manpower and Battle Deaths

Directions: Study the graphs. Then use the information to answer the questions below.

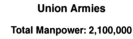
Union Armies
Total Manpower: 2,100,000

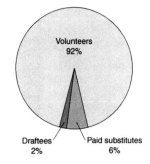

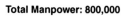
Confederate Armies
Total Manpower: 800,000

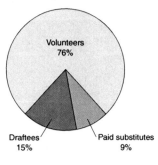

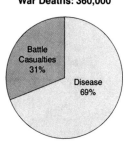
War Deaths: 360,000

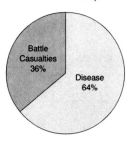
War Deaths: 260,000

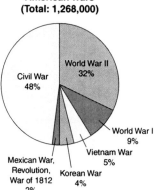
Deaths in Major American Wars
(Total: 1,268,000)

1. How did the majority of soldiers come into the armies? What does that tell you about the soldiers?

_____

2. What was the greatest cause of deaths in both armies? _____

_____

3. Write a sentence comparing the casualties in the Civil War to the casualties in all other major American wars.

_____

© OXFORD UNIVERSITY PRESS

Name _____ **Date** _____

RESOURCE PAGE 7

Geography and the Battle of Gettysburg

Directions: Study the topographical map showing the Battle of Gettysburg. Then use the map and the information in the textbook to answer the questions that follow.

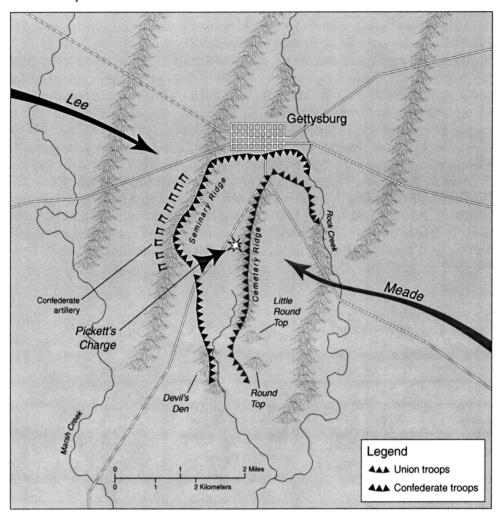

1. Why is it important to control high ground in a battle? What high ground did each side hold at Gettysburg?

_____

_____

2. On the second day, the Confederates almost captured Round Top and Little Round Top. What might have happened to the main Union army on Cemetery Ridge if the Confederates had gained control of these hills?

_____

_____

3. Many historians think that Pickett's Charge was doomed to fail. Looking at the map, why might this be true?

_____

_____

Name _____   Date _____

RESOURCE PAGE 8

The Gettysburg Address: A Closer Look

Directions: With a partner, read Lincoln's Gettysburg Address. Then answer the questions that follow to analyze what Lincoln said and how he said it.

> Four score and seven years ago our fathers brought forth on this continent, a new nation, conceived in Liberty, and dedicated to the proposition that all men are created equal.
>
> Now we are engaged in a great civil war, testing whether that nation, or any nation so conceived, and so dedicated, can long endure. We are met on a great battlefield of that war. We have come to dedicate a portion of that field as a final resting place for those who here gave their lives that that nation might live. It is altogether fitting and proper that we should do this.
>
> But, in a larger sense, we can not dedicate—we can not consecrate—we can not hallow this ground. The brave men, living and dead, who struggled here, have consecrated it, far above our poor power to add or detract. The world will little note, nor long remember, what we say here, but it can never forget what they did here. It is for us the living, rather, to be dedicated here to the unfinished work which they who fought here have thus far so nobly advanced. It is rather for us to be here dedicated to the great task remaining before us—that from these honored dead we take increased devotion to that cause for which they gave the last full measure of devotion—that we highly resolve that these dead shall not have died in vain—that this nation, under God, shall have a new birth of freedom—and that government of the people, by the people, for the people, shall not perish from the earth.

1. A *score* equals 20. To what year does Lincoln take us back? Why?

_____

_____

2. To what is Lincoln referring when he says the United States was born "dedicated to the proposition that all men are created equal"?

_____

_____

3. According to Lincoln, what is the Civil War testing?

_____

_____

4. What advice does Lincoln give? What does he want them to realize about the purpose of the Civil War?

_____

_____

5. According to Lincoln, what might happen if the North loses the Civil War?

_____

_____

RESOURCE PAGE 9

The Yankees Are Coming!

Directions: Dolly Sumner Lunt Burge was a widowed plantation owner near Covington, Georgia. She, her nine-year-old daughter Sadai, and about 100 slaves were in the path of Sherman's March to the Sea. Read these excerpts from her diary. Then follow your teacher's instructions.

November 16, 1864—Paid seven dollars a pound for coffee…five dollars for ten cents' worth of flax thread, six dollars for pins, and forty dollars for a bunch of factory thread.…On our way home we met Brother Evans…who inquired if we had heard that the Yankees were coming…and that it was reported that the Yankees were on their way to Savannah.…

November 17, 1864—Have been uneasy all day. At night some of the neighbors who had been to town called. They said it was a large force moving very slowly. What shall I do. Where go?

November 19, 1864—I saw some blue-coats coming down the hill.…I walked to the gate. There they came filing up. I hastened back to my frightened servants and told them that they had better hide.…Like demons [the Yankees] rush in! My yards are full. To my smoke-house, my dairy, pantry, kitchen, cellar, like famished wolves they come, breaking locks and whatever is in their way. The thousand pounds of meat in my smoke-house is gone in a twinkling, my flour, my meat, my lard, butter, eggs, pickles…all are gone. My eighteen fat turkeys, my hens, chickens, fowls, young pigs, are shot down in my yard.…

Alas! little did I think while trying to save my house from plunder and fire that they were forcing my boys from home at the point of the bayonet. One, Newton, jumped into bed in his cabin, and declared himself sick. Another crawled under the floor—a lame boy he was—but they pulled him out, placed him on a horse, and drove him off.…Jack came crying to me, the big tears coursing down his cheeks, saying they were making him go.…[They] threatened to shoot him if he did not go; so poor Jack had to yield.…[The soldiers were] cursing them and saying that "Jeff Davis wanted to put them in his army, [but] that they should not fight for him, but for the Union."…My poor boys! My poor boys! What unknown trials are before you! Their parents are with me, and how sadly they lament the loss of their boys.…

Sherman himself and a greater portion of his army passed my house that day. All day…they were passing not only in front of my house, but from behind; they tore down my garden palings, made a road through my back-yard and lot field, driving their stock and riding through, tearing down my fences and desolating my home—wantonly doing it when there was no necessity for it.…[That night] the heavens were lit up with flames from burning buildings. Dinnerless and supperless as we were, it was nothing in comparison with the fear of being driven out homeless to the dreary woods.…[That night] I could not close my eyes, but kept walking to and fro, watching the fires in the distance and dreading the approaching day, which, I feared, as they had not all passed, would be but a continuation of horrors.

RESOURCE PAGE 10

O Captain! My Captain!

Directions: The following poem is Walt Whitman's tribute to Abraham Lincoln. Read and enjoy the poem. Then answer the questions below.

O Captain! My Captain!

O Captain! my Captain, our fearful trip is done,
The ship has weather'd every rack, the prize we
    sought is won,
The port is near, the bells I hear, the people all exult-
    ing,
While follow eyes the steady keel, the vessel grim
    and daring;

But O heart! heart! heart!
O the bleeding drops of red,
Where on the deck my Captain lies,
Fallen cold and dead.

O Captain! my Captain! rise up and hear the bells;
Rise up—for you the flag is flung—for you the
    bugle trills,
For you bouquets and ribbon'd wreaths—for you
    the shores a-crowding,
For you they call, the swaying mass, their eager faces
    turning:

Here Captain! dear father!
The arm beneath your head!
It is some dream that on the deck,
You've fallen cold and dead.

My Captain does not answer, his lips are pale and
    still,
My father does not feel my arm, he has no pulse nor
    will,
The ship is anchor'd safe and sound, its voyage
    closed and done,
From fearful trip the victor ship comes in with
    object won;

Exult O shores, and ring O bells!
But I with mournful tread,
Walk the deck my Captain lies,
Fallen cold and dead.

1. Who is the Captain?

_____

2. What "fearful trip" has finished and what "prize" was won?

_____

3. What has happened to the Captain just as victory was won?

_____

4. What phrases are repeated in the poem? Why do you think they are repeated?

_____

_____

5. How does the poem capture the mood of the country after Lincoln's death?

_____

_____

© OXFORD UNIVERSITY PRESS

RESOURCE PAGE 11

Nat Turner's Rebellion

Read the following two passages. Then follow your teacher's instructions. The first is from the Richmond *Enquirer*, and the second is from "The Confessions of Nat Turner."

"What strikes us as the most remarkable thing in this matter is the horrible ferocity of these monsters. They remind one of a parcel of blood–thirsty wolves rushing down from the Alps; or rather like a former incursion of the Indians upon the white settlements. Nothing is spared; neither age nor sex is respected- the helplessness of women and children pleads in vain for mercy. The danger is thought to be over- but prudence still demands precaution. The lower country should be on the alert. The case of Nat Turner warns us…

"[Nat Turner] was artful, impudent and vindicative [sic], **without any cause or provocation**, that could be assigned… [His group was] mounted to the number of 40 or 50; and with knives and axes-knocking on the head, or cutting the throats of their victims… These wretches are now estimated to have committed sixty-one murders!"

-from the Richmond *Enquirer*

**

"Since the commencement of 1830 I had been living with Mr. Joseph Travis, who was a kind master, and placed the greatest confidence in me; in fact, **I had no cause to complain of his treatment to me**…

"It was quickly agreed we should commence at home (Mr. J. Travis) on that night; and until we had armed and equipped ourselves, and gathered sufficient force, neither age nor sex was to be spared—which was invariably adhered to…

"I took my station in the rear, and, as it was my object to carry terror and devastation wherever we went, I placed fifteen or twenty of the best armed most to be relied on in front, who generally approached the houses as fast as their horses could run. This was for two purposes—to prevent their escape, and strike terror to the inhabitants; on this account I never got to the houses… until the murders were committed, except in one case. I sometimes got in sight in time to see the work of death completed; viewed the mangled bodies as they lay, in silent satisfaction, and immediately started in quest of other victims."

-from "The Confessions of Nat Turner"

RESOURCE PAGE 12

Theodore Weld - American Slavery As It Is (1839)

Directions: Read the passage below, written by abolitionist Theodore Weld. Then, follow your teacher's instructions.

"Reader, you are empannelled as a juror to try a plain case and bring in an honest verdict. The question at issue is not one of law, but of fact—"What is the actual condition
of the slaves in the United States?" A plainer case never went to a jury. Look at it.
Twenty-seven hundred thousand persons in this country, men, women, and children,
are in slavery. Is slavery, as a condition for human beings, good, bad, or indifferent? We
submit the question without argument. You have common sense, and conscience, and
a human heart;—pronounce upon it. You have a wife, or a husband, a child, a father, a
mother, a brother or a sister—make the case your own, make it theirs, and bring in
your verdict...

empannelled-enlisted

pronounce-decide

"We repeat it, every man knows that slavery is a curse. Whoever denies this, his lips
libel his heart. Try him; clank the chains in his ears, and tell him they are for him. Give
him an hour to prepare his wife and children for a life of slavery. Bid him make haste
and get ready their necks for the yoke, and their wrists for the coffle chains, then look
at his pale lips and trembling knees, and you have nature's testimony against slavery.

libel-misrepresent

coffle chains-for tying
slaves together in a row

"Two millions seven hundred thousand persons in these States are in this condition.
They were made slaves and are held such by force, and by being put in fear, and this for
no crime! Reader, what have you to say of such treatment? Is it right, just, benevolent?
Suppose I should seize you, rob you of your liberty, drive you into the field, and make
you work without pay as long as you live, would that be justice and kindness, or mon-
strous injustice and cruelty? Now, every body knows that the slaveholders do these
things to the slaves every day, and yet it is stoutly affirmed that they treat them well
and kindly, and that their tender regard for their slaves restrains the masters from
inflicting cruelties upon them...

What! slaveholders talk of treating men well, and yet not only rob them of all they get,
and as fast as they get it, but rob them of themselves, also; their very hands and feet, all
their muscles, and limbs, and senses, their bodies and minds, their time and liberty
and earnings, their free speech and rights of conscience, their right to acquire knowledge, and property, and reputation;—and yet they, who plunder them of all these,
would fain make us believe that their soft hearts ooze out so lovingly toward their
slaves that they always keep them well housed and well clad, never push them too hard
in the field, never make their dear backs smart, nor let their dear stomachs get
empty...

fain-willingly

"All these pleas, and scores of others, are bruited in every corner of the free States; and
who that hath eyes to see, has not sickened at the blindness that saw not, at the palsy of
heart that felt not, or at the cowardice and sycophancy that dared not expose such
shallow fallacies. We are not to be turned from our purpose by such vapid babblings."

bruited-spread
palsy-sickness
sycophancy-servility
fallacies-lies
vapid-empty

USING THE
MAP RESOURCE PAGES

These maps are black and white versions of the maps in the Atlas section of *War, Terrible War*.

Free States and Slave States, 1861
Project suggestion: Use this map with the reproducible map described below to study the changing geographic limits of slavery in the U.S. This map shows boundaries of legalized slavery in 1861, at the beginning of the Civil War.

Northern Economies
Southern Economies
Project suggestion: Discuss with students what most people did for a living in 1860. Have students notice and describe regional difference in economy and lifestyle.

These maps are provided for use with class projects and activities:

Reproducible Civil War Room map*
Project suggestion: Use this map with the Civil War Room ongoing activity described on TG page 32. Have students mark important battle locations, events, capitals and troop movements from Harpers Ferry through Appomattox as they read the book.

Reproducible Eastern US relief map*
Project suggestion: Use this map to chart the Underground Railroad routes found in the "Geography Connections" activity on page 31.
Or, use this map to draw General Scott's Anaconda plan, described in the "Geography Connections" activity on TG page 45.

Reproducible Blank U.S. Political map w/ state boundaries
Project suggestion: Reproduce several copies of this map and have students trace the changing geographic limits of slavery in the U.S. from the Missouri Compromise through the Emancipation Proclamation. Use this together with the "Free States and Slave States, 1861" map, above, and with "Using Maps" project on TG page 34, and "Geography Connections" activity on TG page 63.

* These maps are also printed in each Student Study Guide for *War, Terrible War*.

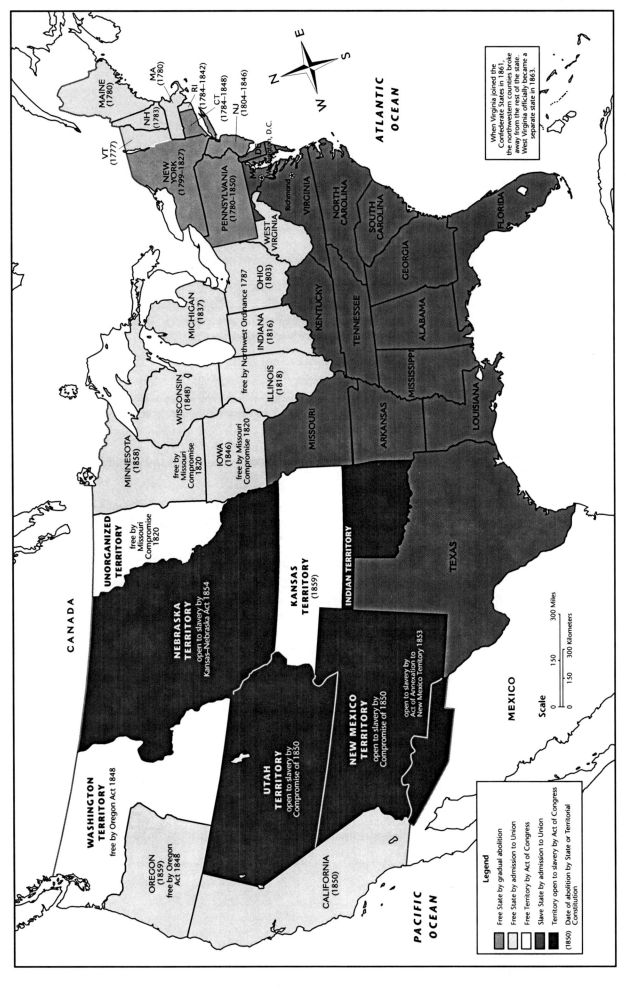

When Virginia joined the Confederate States in 1861, the northwestern counties broke away from the rest of the state. West Virginia officially became a separate state in 1863.

MAINE (1780)
MA (1780)
RI (1784–1842)
CT (1784–1848)
NJ (1804–1846)
VT (1777)
NH (1783)
NEW YORK (1799–1827)
PENNSYLVANIA (1780–1850)
Washington, D.C.
MD
DE
WEST VIRGINIA
VIRGINIA
Richmond
NORTH CAROLINA
SOUTH CAROLINA
GEORGIA
FLORIDA
ATLANTIC OCEAN

OHIO (1803)
free by Northwest Ordinance 1787
MICHIGAN (1837)
INDIANA (1816)
ILLINOIS (1818)
KENTUCKY
TENNESSEE
ALABAMA
MISSISSIPPI
LOUISIANA
ARKANSAS
MISSOURI

WISCONSIN (1848)
MINNESOTA (1858)
IOWA (1846)
free by Missouri Compromise 1820
free by Missouri Compromise 1820
free by Missouri Compromise 1820

UNORGANIZED TERRITORY
NEBRASKA TERRITORY
open to slavery by Kansas–Nebraska Act 1854
KANSAS TERRITORY (1859)
INDIAN TERRITORY
TEXAS
MEXICO

WASHINGTON TERRITORY
free by Oregon Act 1848
OREGON (1859) free by Oregon Act 1848
UTAH TERRITORY
open to slavery by Compromise of 1850
NEW MEXICO TERRITORY
open to slavery by Compromise of 1850
open to slavery by Act of Annexation to New Mexico Territory 1853
CALIFORNIA (1850)

CANADA

PACIFIC OCEAN

Scale
0   150   300 Miles
0   150   300 Kilometers

Legend

Free State by gradual abolition

Free State by admission to Union

Free Territory by Act of Congress

Slave State by admission to Union

Territory open to slavery by Act of Congress

(1850) Date of abolition by State or Territorial Constitution

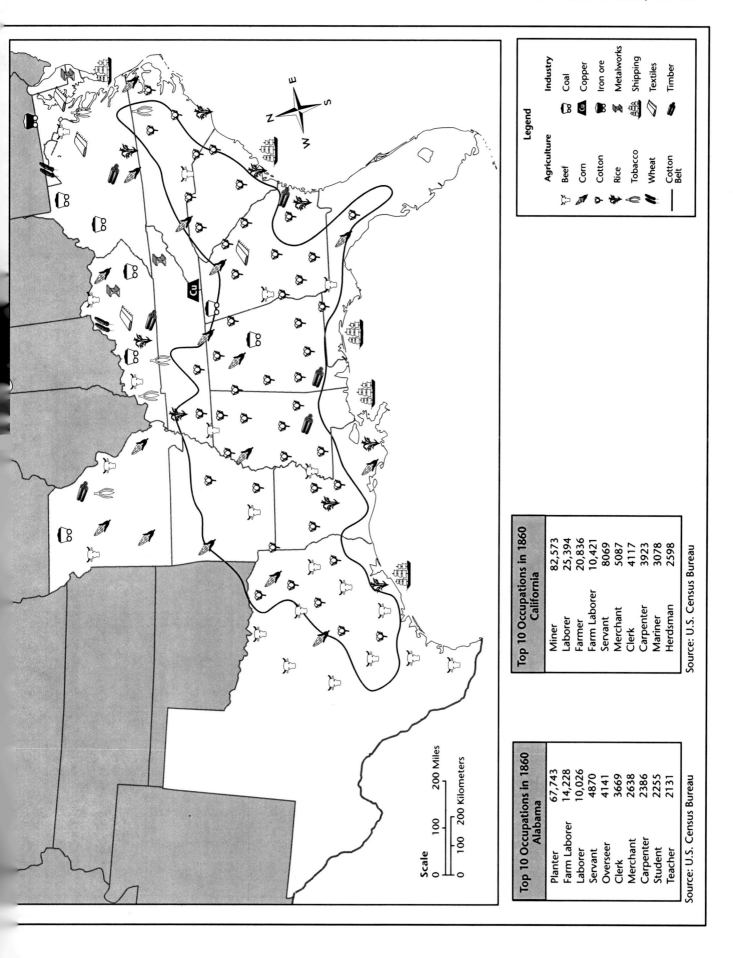

Scale

0   100   200 Miles

0   100   200 Kilometers

Legend

Agriculture

Beef
Corn
Cotton
Rice
Tobacco
Wheat
Cotton Belt

Industry

Coal
Copper
Iron ore
Metalworks
Shipping
Textiles
Timber

Top 10 Occupations in 1860 California	
Miner	82,573
Laborer	25,394
Farmer	20,836
Farm Laborer	10,421
Servant	8069
Merchant	5087
Clerk	4117
Carpenter	3923
Mariner	3078
Herdsman	2598

Source: U.S. Census Bureau

Top 10 Occupations in 1860 Alabama	
Planter	67,743
Farm Laborer	14,228
Laborer	10,026
Servant	4870
Overseer	4141
Clerk	3669
Merchant	2638
Carpenter	2386
Student	2255
Teacher	2131

Source: U.S. Census Bureau

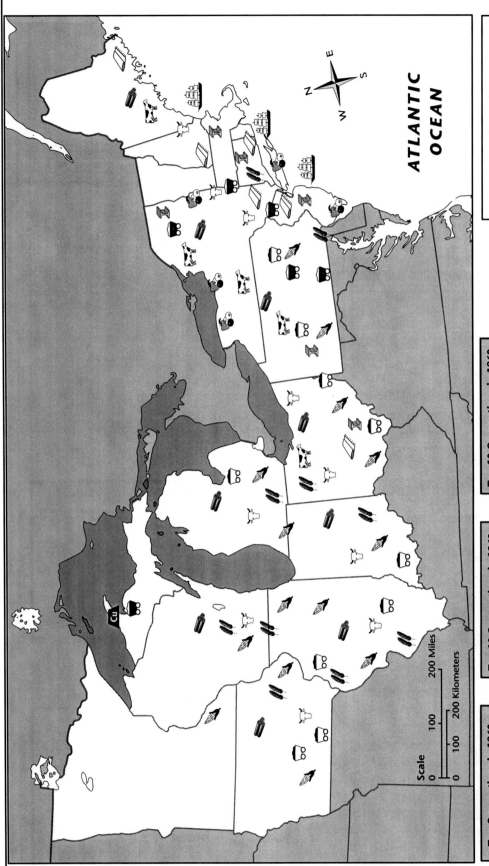

ATLANTIC OCEAN

Legend

Agriculture		Industry	
Beef		Coal	
Corn		Copper	
Dairy		Iron ore	
Orchard fruit		Metalworks	
Wheat		Shipping	
		Textiles	
		Timber	

Source: U.S. Census Bureau

Top 10 Occupations in 1860
Ohio

Farmer	223,485
Laborer	78,523
Farm Laborer	76,484
Servant	33,679
Carpenter	21,571
Shoemaker	11,396
Clerk	10,962
Teacher	10,591
Blacksmith	10,088
Merchant	8602

Top 10 Occupations in 1860
New York

Farmer	254,786
Laborer	159,077
Servant	155,282
Farm Laborer	115,728
Clerk	49,597
Carpenter	38,897
Tailor	33,295
Shoemaker	25,753
Merchant	21,677
Seamstress	18,841

Top Occupations in 1860
National Average

Rounded to nearest percent	
Farmer	29%
Laborer	12%
Farm Laborer	10%
Servant	7%
Carpenter	3%
Clerk	2%
Shoemaker	2%
Merchant	1%
Miner	1%
Blacksmith	1%
Teacher	1%
Tailor	1%

Scale

0   100   200 Miles

0   100   200 Kilometers

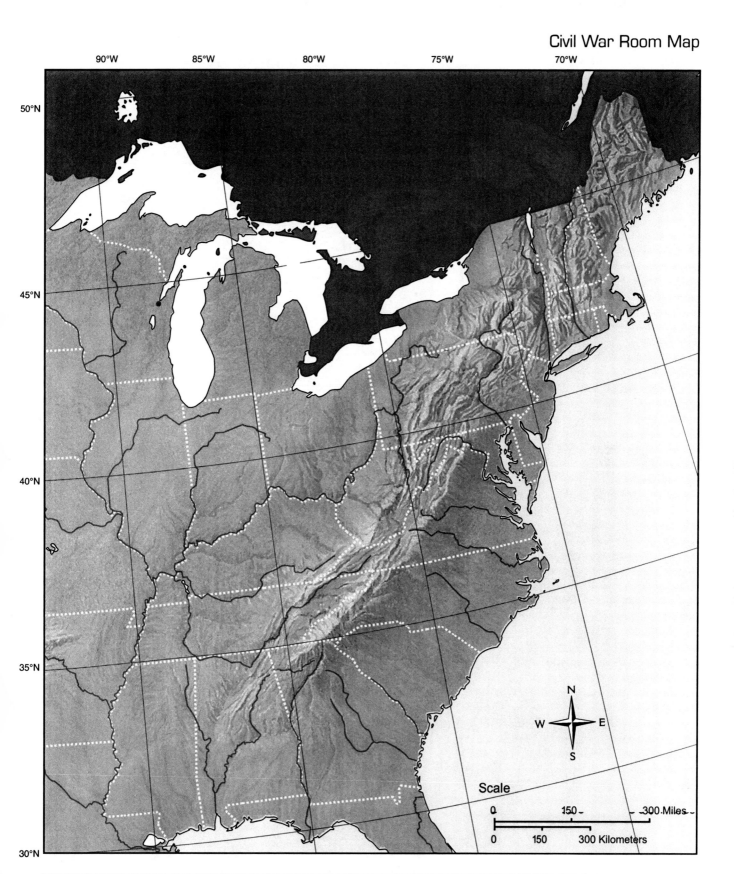

50°N

45°N

40°N

35°N

30°N

90°W   85°W   80°W   75°W   70°W

N
W   E
S

Scale

0   150   300 Miles

0   150   300 Kilometers

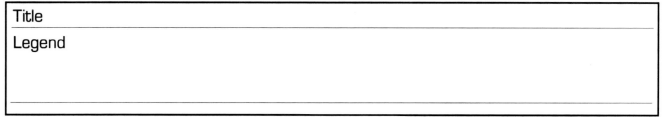

Title _____

Legend

_____

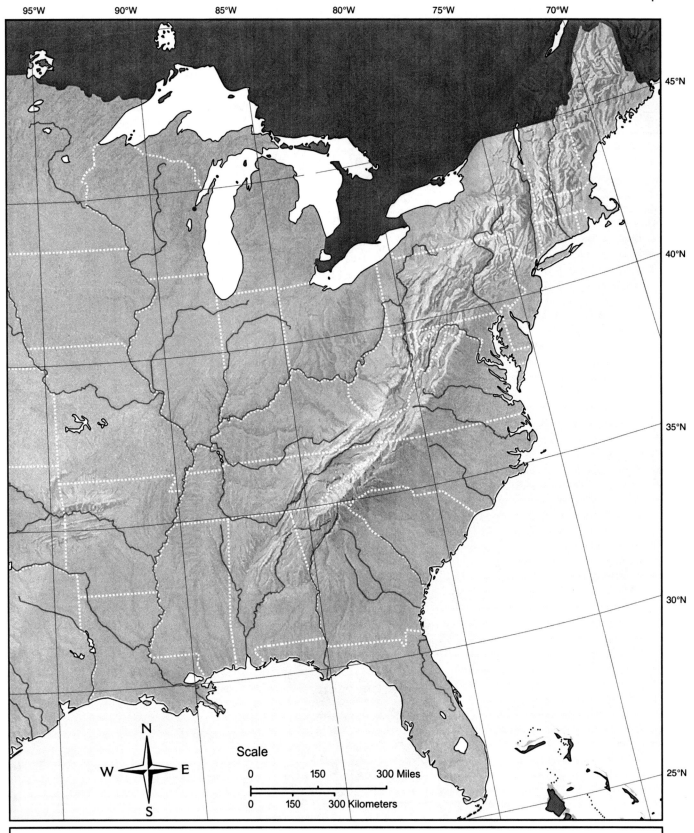

95°W   90°W   85°W   80°W   75°W   70°W

45°N

40°N

35°N

30°N

25°N

N
W   E
S

Scale

0   150   300 Miles

0   150   300 Kilometers

Title

Legend

Blank US Political Map w/ State Borders

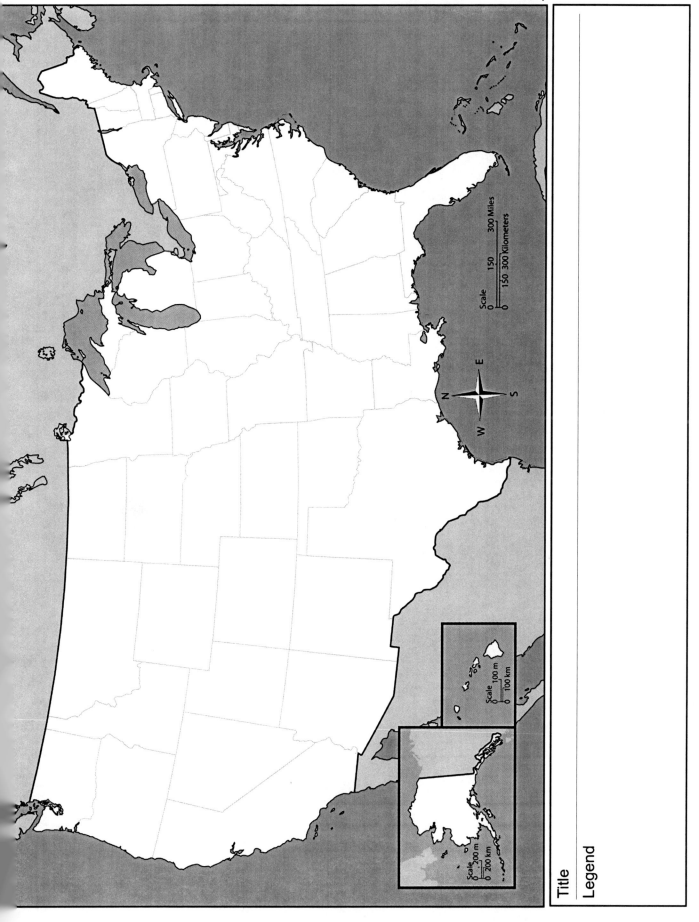

Title

Legend

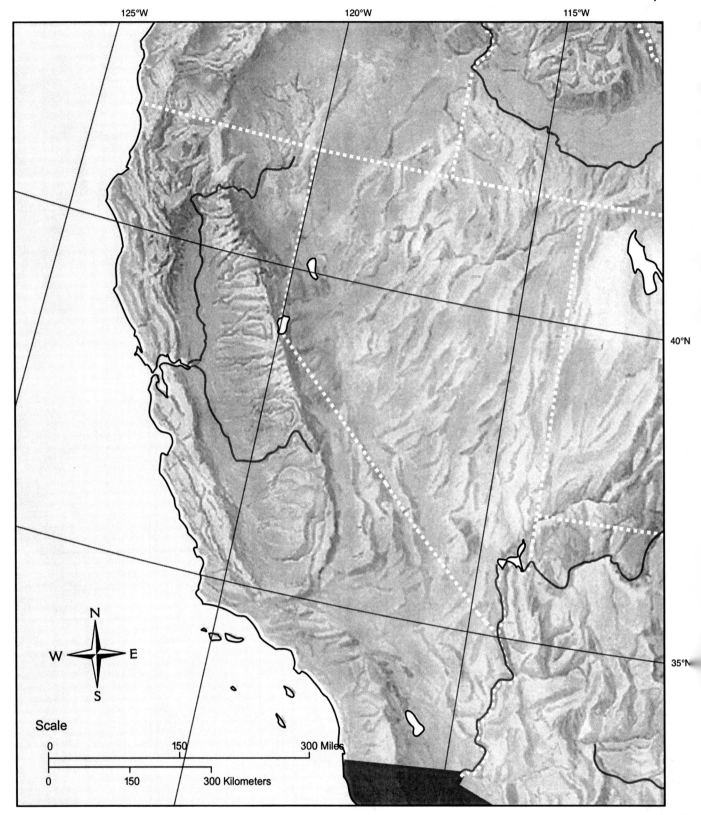

125°W 120°W 115°W

40°N

35°N

N
W E
S

Scale

0   150   300 Miles

0   150   300 Kilometers

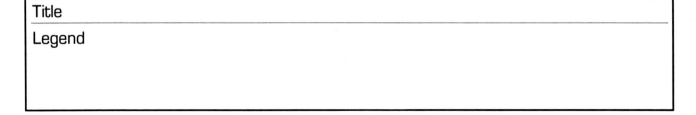

Title

Legend

SCORING RUBRIC

The reproducibles on the following pages have been adapted from this rubric for use as handouts and a student self-scoring activity, with added focus on planning, cooperation, revision and presentation. You may wish to tailor the self-scoring activity—for example, asking students to comment on how low scores could be improved, or focusing only on specific rubric points. Use the Library/Media Center Research Log to help students focus and evaluate their research for projects and assignments.

As with any rubric, you should introduce and explain the rubric before students begin their assignments. The more thoroughly your students understand how they will be evaluated, the better prepared they will be to produce projects that fulfill your expectations.

	ORGANIZATION	CONTENT	ORAL/WRITTEN CONVENTIONS	GROUP PARTICIPATION
4	• Clearly addresses all parts of the writing task. • Demonstrates a clear understanding of purpose and audience. • Maintains a consistent point of view, focus, and organizational structure, including the effective use of transitions. • Includes a clearly presented central idea with relevant facts, details, and/or explanations.	• Demonstrates that the topic was well researched. • Uses only information that was essential and relevant to the topic. • Presents the topic thoroughly and accurately. • Reaches reasonable conclusions clearly based on evidence.	• Contains few, if any, errors in grammar, punctuation, capitalization, or spelling. • Uses a variety of sentence types. • Speaks clearly, using effective volume and intonation.	• Demonstrated high levels of participation and effective decision making. • Planned well and used time efficiently. • Demonstrated ability to negotiate opinions fairly and reach compromise when needed. • Utilized effective visual aids.
3	• Addresses all parts of the writing task. • Demonstrates a general understanding of purpose and audience. • Maintains a mostly consistent point of view, focus, and organizational structure, including the effective use of some transitions. • Presents a central idea with mostly relevant facts, details, and/or explanations.	• Demonstrates that the topic was sufficiently researched. • Uses mainly information that was essential and relevant to the topic. • Presents the topic accurately but leaves some aspects unexplored. • Reaches reasonable conclusions loosely related to evidence.	• Contains some errors in grammar, punctuation, capitalization, or spelling. • Uses a variety of sentence types. • Speaks somewhat clearly, using effective volume and intonation.	• Demonstrated good participation and decision making with few distractions. • Planning and used its time acceptably. • Demonstrated ability to negotiate opinions and compromise with little aggression or unfairness.
2	• Addresses only parts of the writing task. • Demonstrates little understanding of purpose and audience. • Maintains an inconsistent point of view, focus, and/or organizational structure, which may include ineffective or awkward transitions that do not unify important ideas. • Suggests a central idea with limited facts, details, and/or explanations.	• Demonstrates that the topic was minimally researched. • Uses a mix of relevant and irrelevant information. • Presents the topic with some factual errors and leaves some aspects unexplored. • Reaches conclusions that do not stem from evidence presented in the project.	• Contains several errors in grammar, punctuation, capitalization, or spelling. These errors may interfere with the reader's understanding of the writing. • Uses little variety in sentence types. • Speaks unclearly or too quickly. May interfere with the audience's understanding of the project.	• Demonstrated uneven participation or was often off-topic. Task distribution was lopsided. • Did not show a clear plan for the project, and did not use time well. • Allowed one or two opinions to dominate the activity, or had trouble reaching a fair consensus.
1	• Addresses only one part of the writing task. • Demonstrates no understanding of purpose and audience. • Lacks a point of view, focus, organizational structure, and transitions that unify important ideas. • Lacks a central idea but may contain marginally related facts, details, and/or explanations.	• Demonstrates that the topic was poorly researched. • Does not discriminate relevant from irrelevant information. • Presents the topic incompletely, with many factual errors. • Did not reach conclusions.	• Contains serious errors in grammar, punctuation, capitalization, or spelling. These errors interfere with the reader's understanding of the writing. • Uses no sentence variety. • Speaks unclearly. The audience must struggle to understand the project.	• Demonstrated poor participation by the majority of the group. Tasks were completed by a small minority. • Failed to show planning or effective use of time. • Was dominated by a single voice, or allowed hostility to derail the project.

NAME _____ **PROJECT** _____

DATE _____

ORGANIZATION & FOCUS	CONTENT	ORAL/WRITTEN CONVENTIONS	GROUP PARTICIPATION

COMMENTS AND SUGGESTIONS

UNDERSTANDING YOUR SCORE

Organization: Your project should be clear, focused on a main idea, and organized. You should use details and facts to support your main idea.

Content: You should use strong research skills. Your project should be thorough and accurate.

Oral/Written Conventions: For writing projects, you should use good composition, grammar, punctuation, and spelling, with a good variety of sentence types. For oral projects, you should engage the class using good public speaking skills.

Group Participation: Your group should cooperate fairly and use its time well to plan, assign and revise the tasks involved in the project.

NAME _____ **GROUP MEMBERS** _____

_____

_____

_____

Use this worksheet to describe your project by finishing the sentences below.
For individual projects and writing assignments, use the "How I did" section.
For group projects, use both "How I did" and "How we did" sections.

The purpose of this project is to :

Scoring Key = **4** – extremely well
3 – well
2 – could have been better
1 – not well at all

HOW I DID

I understood the purpose and requirements for this project…

I planned and organized my time and work…

This project showed clear organization that emphasized the central idea…

I supported my point with details and description…

I polished and revised this project…

I utilized correct grammar and good writing/speaking style…

Overall, this project met its purpose…

HOW WE DID

We divided up tasks…

We cooperated and listened to each other…

We talked through what we didn't understand…

We used all our time to make this project the best it could be…

Overall, as a group we worked together…

I contributed and cooperated with the team…

LIBRARY / MEDIA CENTER RESEARCH LOG

NAME _____

DUE DATE _____

What I Need to Find

I need to use:
- ☐ primary sources.
- ☐ secondary

Places I Know to Look

Brainstorm: Other Sources and Places to Look

WHAT I FOUND

Title/Author/Location (call # or URL)

| | Book/Periodical | Website | Other | Primary Source | Secondary Source | Suggestion | Library Catalog | Browsing | Internet Search | Web link | How I Found it | helpful | relevant |

OUTLINE

MAIN IDEA: _____

_____

_____

      DETAIL: _____

_____

      DETAIL: _____

_____

      DETAIL: _____

_____

MAIN IDEA: _____

_____

_____

      DETAIL: _____

_____

      DETAIL: _____

_____

      DETAIL: _____

_____

Name _____ Date _____

MAIN IDEA MAP

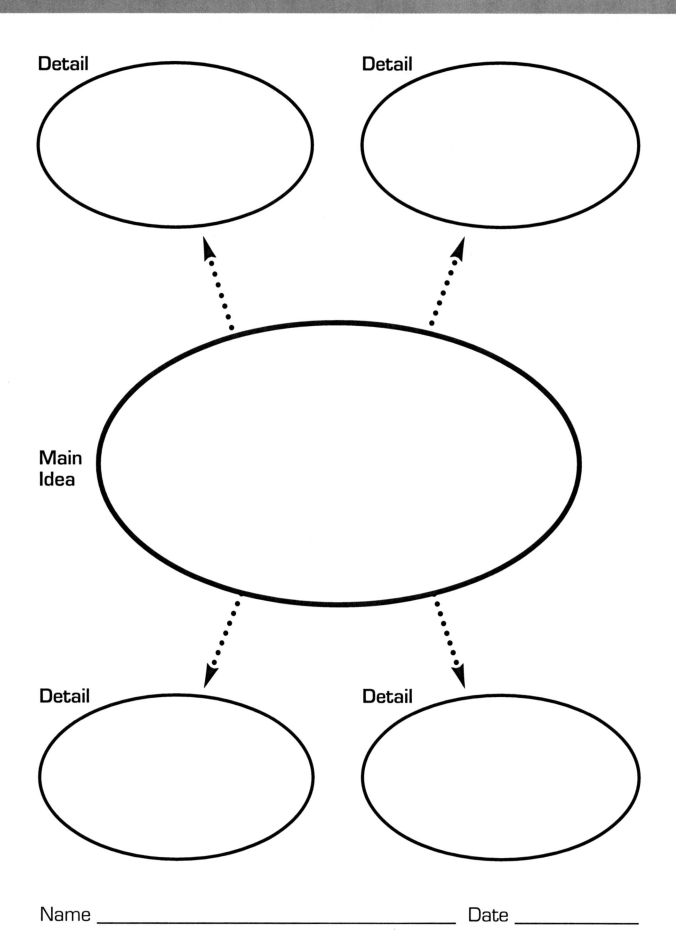

Detail

Detail

Main
Idea

Detail

Detail

Name _____ Date _____

KWL CHART

K	W	L
What I Know	What I Want to Know	What I Learned

Name _____

Date _____

VENN DIAGRAM

Write differences in the circles. Write similarities where the circles overlap.

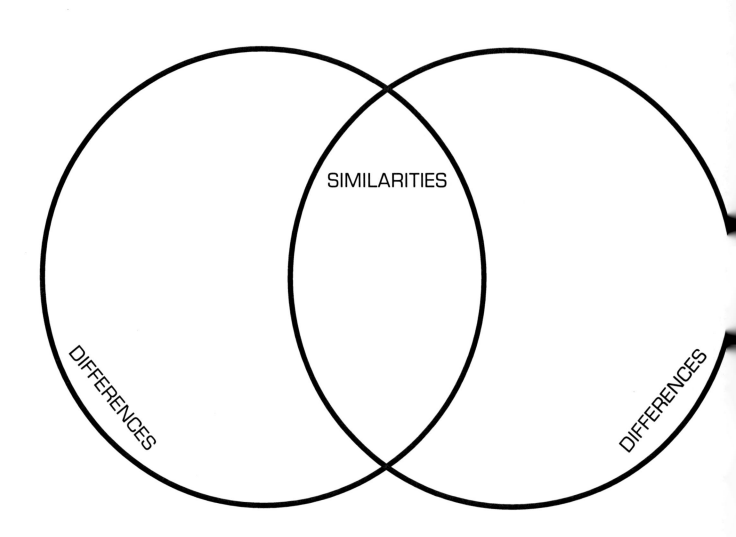

SIMILARITIES

DIFFERENCES

DIFFERENCES

Name _____ Date _____

TIMELINE

DATE

EVENT   Draw lines to connect the event to the correct year on the timeline.

Name _____ Date

SEQUENCE OF EVENTS CHART

Event

Next Event

Next Event

Next Event

Next Event

Name _____ Date _____

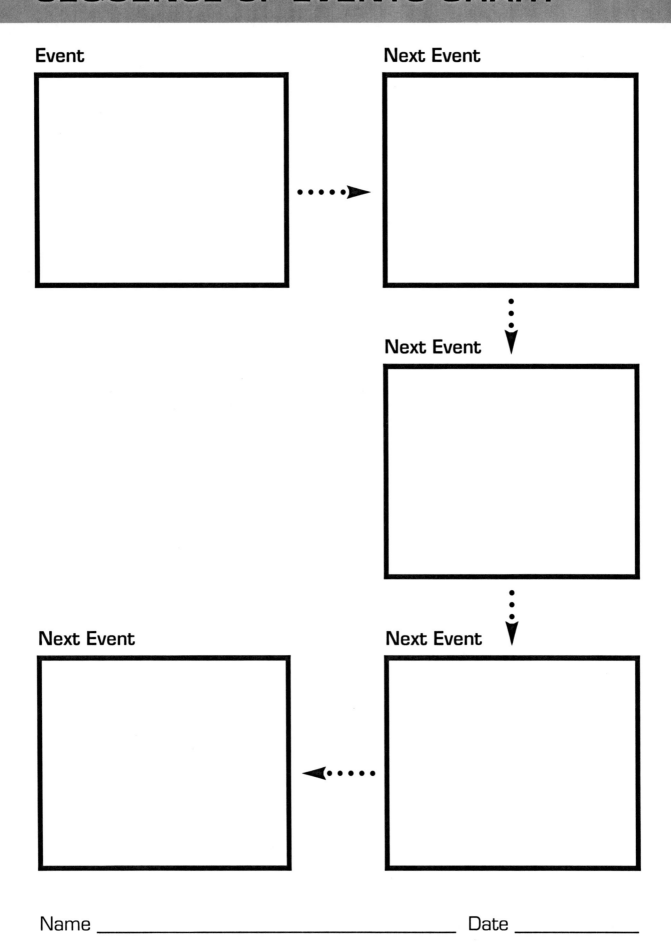

T–CHART

Cause	Effect

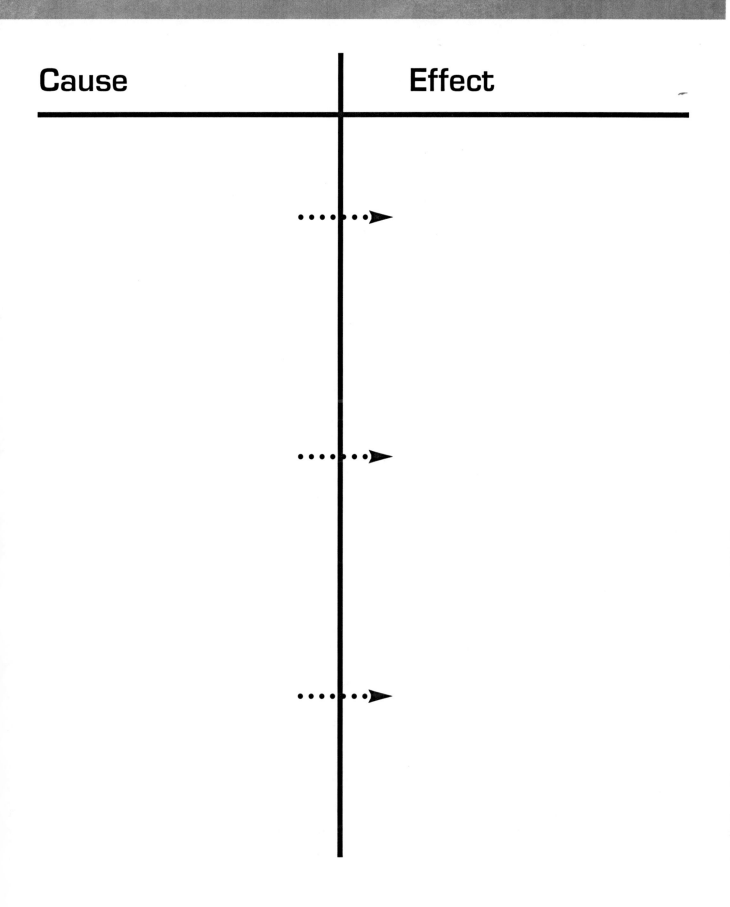

Name _____ Date _____

TEACHING GUIDE
ANSWER KEY

CHECK-UP 1

1. (a) supported a strong Union in earlier secession crisis (b) staunch defender of states' rights (c) early defender of states' rights (d) suggested that the government pay slave owners for slaves and set them free (e) commanded Southern forces at Ft. Sumter (f) stood firm (like a stone wall) at First Bull Run.

2. (a) site of the famous toasts of Jackson and Calhoun (b) site of the arrival of the first Africans, who came as indentured servants (c) first battle of the Civil War (d) site of the first large engagement of Northern and Southern soldiers (e) Confederate Capital.

3. (a) the national government (b) Southern name for slavery (c) the argument that a state can nullify a federal law (d) one who fights to end slavery (e) another name for Confederates (f) another name for Northerners (g) to break away, as the Southern states did in 1861 (h) the holler given by Confederate troops.

4. Postcards should accurately describe or use the name place or term.

5. states rights vs. federalism; slavery vs. liberty.

6. Slavery fueled the Southern economy by providing a source of cheap labor. Also slave owners had an investment in their human "property."

7. Answers should reveal Lincoln's belief that the South had no moral cause for rebellion—i.e., that the use of "independence" was a way of sugarcoating the cause of war.

8. Headlines should reflect the political thinking of each region.

9. Answers should reflect the inexperience of Northern troops and the knowledge that the war would not be easily won.

10. Some students may note that other divisive issues, such as states' rights, stretched back to the Federalist era. Others may argue that all issues—including states' rights—related in some way to slavery.

CHECK-UP 2

1. (a) wrote *Uncle Tom's Cabin*, which created an enormous amount of anti-slavery sentiment (b) an abolitionist and conductor on the Underground Railroad (c) elected President in 1860 and seen by Southerners as a threat to their way of life (d) President of the Confederate States of America and a defender of states' rights (e) polarized the nation with his suicidal raid on Harper's Ferry.

2. (a) where Lincoln was born and spent the first eight years of his life (b) where the Lincoln family lived before moving to Illinois (c) where Lincoln lived and became a lawyer, soldier, businessman, and politician (d) where Lincoln lived after 1838 (e) site of one of the Lincoln-Douglas debates of 1858.

3. (a) secret network that allowed runaway slaves to escape (b) guided runaway slaves North (c) the idea that a state or territory could decide on its own to be a free or a slave state (d) laws that required runaway slaves in the North to be returned to Southern owners (e) people who fought to end slavery.

4. Dialogues should show the efforts of both people to condemn slavery without condemning the people caught up in the system.

5. Most students will agree with Brown, noting Tubman's courage and her "guerrilla" skills. In reality, Tubman greatly admired Brown and wept openly over his death.

6. Paragraphs might mention the current state of the nation(s) and/or a defense of the government that each president represented.

7. Articles will vary, but make sure students understand the national significance of the debates in Illinois.

8. Some students might point out that the Virginia experiment could have shown other states how to free enslaved Africans. Other students might argue that economic costs of abolition were too high for most of the South to pursue.

9. To provoke discussion, you might repeat Tubman's description of Brown: "He was the savior of our people."

10. Although historians still debate this question, most agree that secession would establish a precedent of states' rights that could have undermined the principles of a federal Union.

CHECK-UP 3

1. Encourage students to not only identify each character but to give each an interesting, creative role in the play. (a) Lincoln—Union President (b) Davis—Confederate President (c) Scott—Aging Northern commander and strategist (d) McClellan—cautious Union general (e) Grant—aggressive Union general (f) Greenhow—Confederate socialite and spy (g) Stuart—brilliant Confederate cavalry leader (h) Jackson—Almost unbeatable Southern general (i) Lee—Dignified leader of Confederate's Army of Northern Virginia.

2. (a) Confederate capital (b) site of United States Military Academy, which Lee ran before 1861 (c) slave states that stayed in the Union (d) scene of the first fighting of the Civil War.

3. (a) slave states that stayed in the Union; were on the border between North and South (b) speech given by the President at the beginning of his term (c) the separation of Southern states from the federal Union (d) the bottling up of Southern ports by the Union navy (e) General Scott's plan to divide and squeeze the South (f) a loosely organized grouping of autonomous states.

4. The remark was meant to calm fears in the border states and among Northerners still not ready to fight over enslaved Africans. The statement reflected Lincoln's long-standing compromise to accept slavery where it existed, but to stop its spread.

5. The Anaconda Plan was the idea that the South could be cut in two by capturing the Mississippi River, and then squeezed into submission by attacks from the West and North, and by a naval blockade.

6. Letters should stress Grant's attributes as well as characteristics of other Union generals.

7. Answers should reflect the quotes by Lee on pages 70-72.

8. Encourage students to mention two conflicts in their commentaries—the conflict over slavery and the conflict over states' rights.

9. Students should see that people who were willing to go to war for states' rights would not be willing to give up rights to another central government.

10. Most students will probably feel that once soldiers marched it would be impossible to sidestep the issue of slavery any longer. That was, in fact, what Lincoln hoped.

CHECK-UP 4

1. (a) opposing cavalry leaders and son and father-in-law (b) friends and fellow soldiers before the war who would meet as commanding officers later in the war (c) both invented better and more deadly guns (d) Willie was Abe's son who died during the war.

2. (a) allowed soldiers to shoot more accurately and more rapidly at longer distances (b) allowed armies to move farther and faster (c) made communications easier and an army's movements easier to control.

3. (a) to require someone to serve in the armed forces (b) precursor to baseball (c) a game played with a tin can or block of wood (d) Southern "delicacy" during the war (e) new rifle loaded in back (f) developed a single-shot breech-loading rifle (g) cannons (h) music played by bugler to announce lights out.

4. Sample freedoms expanded or strengthened by the Civil War include equality of opportunity, liberty under the law, right to one's own labor.

5. Lectures should include mention of new weapons, a decline in the importance of hand-to-hand combat, rise of total war, and the involvement of new technology such as railroads and the telegraph.

6. Students might name some of the horrors of war. They might also note anger at those able to "buy" their way out of the fighting.

7. Students should note the independent spirit of the recruits—a spirit that drove them to fight harder. Mercenaries fight for money; free soldiers fight for their beliefs.

8. He was a victim of the poor sanitary practices of wartime.

9. Lead students to understand that the presidency forces a person to function in public regardless of individual losses.

10. Answers should reflect the growth of democracy and constitutional reform that has strengthened our nation.

CHECK-UP 5

1. (a) Union general who was reluctant to fight (b) p. 97, Union naval officer who captured New Orleans and the mouth of the Mississippi River (c) Union nurse and founder of the Red Cross (d) all-black regiment that proved valor of black troops during assault on Fort Wagner (e) suicidal attack by Confederates on Northern defenses at Gettysburg (f) Union commander who shined in the West and eventually defeated Lee (g) Union commander of armies that captured Atlanta and brought total war to Georgia and the Carolinas (h) Union commander whose destruction of the Shenandoah Valley greatly weakened the Confederates

2. (a) the boundary between North and South and the location of Washington, D.C. (b) the site of McClellan's Peninsular campaign (c) site of the battle of the ironclads (d) site of the bloodiest single day of the war (e) site of 54th Massachusetts' famous assault (f) site of a suicidal assault of Northern troops on Southern defenses (g) Southern stronghold on the Mississippi captured by Grant on July 4, 1863 (h) site of the most important battle of the war

3. (a) old ships often sunk in waterways to block passage of enemy ships (b) Lincoln's declaration of freedom for the slaves in rebel territory—redefined the purpose of the war (c) name given to slaves who were freed by the Northern army (d) Union delicacy (e) destruction of both military and civilian targets (f) soldiers who ran away from service.

4. Possible response: To move decisively and quickly. Don't repeat the delays of McClellan or Meade.

5. Eulogies should reflect the genuine mourning and admiration felt by Lee. Lee might urge soldiers to honor Jackson by fighting with renewed valor.

6. Lyrics will vary, but should capture the hope that the end of the war will also mean the end of slavery.

7. The South sought to wear the North out. The North sought a quick end to the war.

8. Responses should note the approval of Jefferson. Reasons should stress the similarity in the ideas of the Declaration and the Gettysburg Address.

9. Students might note the need to end the ongoing war. Also, Lincoln needed to think of plans for peace and ways to help enslaved Africans make the transition to freedom.

10. Reasons should mirror ideas mentioned by the author. Students should support their opinions with well-reasoned arguments. You might encourage them to do this by considering the definition of a revolution

CHECK-UP 6

1. (a) Lincoln, was president during the Civil War and ended slavery (b) Grant, led the Union to victory over the South, but gave gentle terms of surrender (c) Parker, was an Iroquois who became a trusted Union officer (d) Beecher, was a leading minister and abolitionist (e) Rock, was the first African American recognized in Congress (f) Chase, was Chief Justice of the Supreme Court

2. (a) site of nine-month siege by Grant's troops that ended the war (b) Union headquarters near Richmond at the end of the war, site of a meeting between Grant, Lincoln, and Sherman to discuss treatment of the South after the war (c) burned as it was abandoned by the Confederate government and army at the end of the war (d) site of Lee's surrender to Grant (e) area where Confederate troops laid down their weapons

3. (a) the reuniting and rebuilding of the country (b) prohibited slavery (c) gave equal protection of the law to all Americans (d) gave all citizens the right to vote; The three amendments set the tone for Reconstruction.

4. Answers will vary, but most students will focus on the phrase "with malice toward none."

5. Monologues will vary, but may note Lincoln's relief at a Union reunited and/or the price of that Union.

6. Grant did not treat Southerners as traitors.

7. Responses will vary.

8. Obituaries might mirror the words of Elizabeth Keckley.

9. Responses will vary.

10. Responses will vary.

RESOURCE PAGE 1

Students' maps should include the major battles and events of the war and the immediate postwar period and an indication of the Anaconda Plan. Union, Confederate, and border states should be colored.

RESOURCE PAGE 2

This page is to be used with the Student Team Learning Activity for Part 1.

RESOURCE PAGE 3

1. Legree is ordering Tom to whip another slave. Tom is not used to inflicting punishment. He will not whip a fellow human.
2. Legree reacts violently, cursing and whipping Tom.
3. Tom is strong, gentle, and almost spiritual in his convictions.
4. The novel creates a strong emotional reaction in the reader.
5. They are portrayed as being wicked and violent, and slavery is shown to be demeaning to humans.

RESOURCE PAGE 4

1. The two most radical candidates, Lincoln and Breckenridge, won the most states: Lincoln's were all northern, Breckenridge's were all southern. The two conciliatory candidates, Bell and Douglas, won the fewest states.
2. Southerners probably felt that a northern abolitionist had been elected president, and it had been done by the power of northern votes only. This could mean that the federal government would finally pass laws against slavery.

RESOURCE PAGE 5

1. The North's free population was about 16.5 million more than the South's.
2. firearms production
3. Responses will vary.
4. Southerners were defending their own land, only had to outlast the North's desire to fight, felt that the British would come to their aid, believed they had the better soldiers.

RESOURCE PAGE 6

1. The vast majority of soldiers were volunteers, which means they wanted to fight in the war.
2. Most deaths were caused by disease.
3. The Civil War accounts for almost half of all American war deaths.

RESOURCE PAGE 7

1. High ground is the best defensive position. Artillery can fire at the enemy better from high ground. Commanders can see the battlefield better. The Confederates held Seminary Ridge; the Union held Cemetery Ridge, Little Round Top, and Round Top.
2. The Union army might have had to retreat in the face of the enemy holding high ground on its flank and threatening to surround it.
3. The Confederates had to charge across almost a mile of open ground, and then up Cemetery Ridge in the face of deadly Union musket and artillery fire.

RESOURCE PAGE 8

1. 1776; it was the year the Declaration of Independence was signed.
2. The United States was an experiment in democracy.
3. The Civil War was a test of whether a democracy can exist without crumbling because of inherent political tension.
4. He advises his listeners to rededicate themselves to the cause for which the Union soldiers had died—a new birth of freedom for all Americans.
5. Government of the people, by the people, for the people might disappear from the earth.

RESOURCE PAGE 9
This page is to be used with the Student Team Learning Activity for Part 5.

RESOURCE PAGE 10
1. Lincoln.
2. The Civil War; the North has won, the Union is preserved, slavery is ended.
3. The Captain was killed.
4. "O Captain! my Captain!" and "Fallen cold and dead"; the reality of death is in these two lines.
5. Responses will vary, but Whitman hoped to capture the sorrow and pain of the nation as it mourned Lincoln's passing.

STUDENT STUDY GUIDE ANSWER KEY

CHAPTER 1 / CHAPTER 2
Word Bank: 1. gun bore 2. rebel yell, Yankee 3. Rebel, secede.
Critical Thinking: 1. E 2. R 3. Y 4. Y 5. R 6. Y 7. R 8. E.

CHAPTER 3
Word Bank: 1. dialect 2. plantation, overseer.
Parent/Partner 1. probably New York and Pennsylvania 2. west 3. Hudson, Delaware, Allegheny 4. Ohio
Fact or Opinion: 1. F 2. O 3. F 4. O 5. O 6. F.

CHAPTER 4
Word Bank: 1. passengers, Underground Railroad 2. conductors 3. stations 4. civil disobedience.
Parent/Partner: 1. ancient leader of Israelites 2. He was born a slave, but raised as one of Egyptian pharaoh's children 3. Brought about freeing of Israelite slaves in Egypt 4. Hebrew Bible/Christian Old Testament
Primary Sources: 1. safety, cover 2. blanket 3. gather 4. could, would 5. slave catchers

CHAPTER 5 / CHAPTER 6
Word Bank: 1. hooligan 2. blab school 3. mentor 4. injustice 5. policy
Drawing Conclusions: 1.a, b, c 2. a, c 3. a, b.
Primary Sources: 1. custom 2. discuss reasons (owning humans was wrong, cruelty, families separated, etc.) 3. probable answers: it was a disruptive system, bad for economic growth, caused divisiveness.

CHAPTER 7
Word Bank: 1. popular sovereignty 2. fugitive slave law 3. abolitionist, despotism.
Making Inferences: 1. D 2. L 3. L 4. D 6. D 7. L.
Primary Source: 1. freedom 2. power 3. desire for freedom unites people 4. end slavery

CHAPTER 8
Parent/Partner: 1. probably down the Mississippi River through Missouri and Arkansas 2. east 3. Ohio, Mississippi
Sequence of Events: 7, 1, 8, 2, 6, 3, 4, 5
Primary Sources: 1. arrogant 2. poor 3. Ask students to read answers aloud. Discuss

CHAPTER 9
Word Bank: 1. It was illegal to import slaves after 1808. 2. Slaves who ran away were called "fugitives." 3. Answers will vary
Main Idea: 1. c 2. a 3. c.

CHAPTER 10
Word Bank: 1. treason 2. guerilla war 3. martyr 4. strategic
Sequence of Events: 6, 3, 2, 1, 5, 7, 8, 4
Primary Sources: 1. attacked 2. does not like them. 3. discuss

CHAPTER 11
Word Bank: 1. per capita 2. shinplaster 3. industrial hub 4. secede.
Drawing Conclusions: 1. C 2. C 3. U 4. U 5. C 6. C 7. C.
Primary Sources: 1. Revolution 2. country was meant to be whole not separate 3.music and connection

CHAPTER 12
Word Bank: 1. blockade 2. blockade runner 3. Anaconda Plan.
Fact or Opinion: 1. F 2. O 3. F 4. O 5. F 6. O 7. O 8. F.
Map: 1. Charleston, Savannah 2. Kentucky, Missouri 3. Maryland, Delaware.

CHAPTER 13
Word Bank: 1. patriarch 2. invincibility.
Making Inferences: 1.J 2. J 3. J 4. L 5. J 6. L.
Primary Sources: 1. armed force 2. because states have seceded 3. attraction

CHAPTER 14
Word Bank: 1. feudal 2. Articles of Confederation.
Drawing Conclusions: 1. b, c 2. b, c 3. a, c 4. a, b.
Primary Sources: 1. dislikes them 2. Confederacy 3. easier to rule

CHAPTER 15
Word Bank: 1. antebellum 2. pastoral 3. democracy 4. class society
Making Inferences: 1. E 2. S 3. N 4. S 5. S 6. N 7. E.
Primary Sources: 1. America 2. class society 3. immigrants.

CHAPTER 16
Word Bank: 1. conscription, draft 2. slosh 3. breech loading
Main Idea: 1. b 2. a 3. c.
Primary Source: 1. dislikes it 2. pride and valor gone 3. unhappiness.

CHAPTER 17
Word Bank: 1. hayseed 2. compassion
Fact or Opinion: 1. F 2. F 3. O 4. F 5. O 6. F 7. O
Primary Sources: 1. an angel (discuss meaning) 2. God "called him home," "heaven," 3. no war, disease, or death.

CHAPTER 18
Word Bank: 1. ruse 2. peninsula 3. campaign.
Sequence of Events: 7, 3, 5, 6, 1, 2, 4, 8.
All Over the Map: 1. c 2. a 3. b 4. east (southeast)

CHAPTER 19
Parent/Partner: 1. Tennessee River 2. Potomac River 3. Tennessee: Chattanooga, Chickamauga, Shiloh, Fort Henry, Fort Donelson; Potomac: Antietam
Map: 1. Tennessee, discuss (use other maps to show Tennessee River.) 2. supply transport, divide Confederacy; 3. supply, invasion route to North; 4. two capitals near each other.

CHAPTER 20
Main Idea: 1. a 2. c 3. c.
Primary Sources: 1. Emancipation Proclamation 2. Union soldiers 3. Confederates 4. United States.

CHAPTER 21
Fact or Opinion: 1. O 2. F 3. O 4. F 5. O 6. O 7. F 8.O.
Primary Sources: 1. country is at war 2. soldiers 3. African Americans.

CHAPTER 22 / CHAPTER 23
Word Bank: 1. total war 2. hardtack 3. cavalry.
Sequence of Events: 3, 5, 1, 2, 4, 6, 8, 7
Primary Sources: 1. fought 2. bunched together 3. gunpowder is black when it fires

CHAPTER 24
Word Bank: 1. siege 2. deserter.
Parent/Partner: 1. Gettysburg; 2. Vicksburg; 3. Victory at Vicksburg allowed Union army to control the Mississippi River.
Primary Sources: 1. building burning from shelling 2. noise, fear 3. artillery projectiles
Writing: Have students read diary entries aloud

CHAPTER 25
Word Bank: 1. orator. 2. score
Drawing Conclusions: 1.a, b; 2. a, c; 3. b, c.
Primary Sources: 1. win the war 2. preserving the Union 3. to give one's life for one's country.

CHAPTER 26
Word Bank: 1. a 2. b 3. c.
Parent/Partner: 1. James, York, Rappahannock, Appomattox rivers, Chesapeake Bay; 2. To cut off Southern lines of supply and communication.
Map: 1.b 2. a 3. b 4. a

CHAPTER 27
Word Bank: 1. malice 2. Reconstruction.
Making Inferences: 1.c 2. a 3. c 4. b 5. b.
Primary Sources: 1. pay, food, supplies 2. after (discuss "up") 3. dislikes, makes fun of them 4. no funds.

CHAPTER 28
Word Bank: 1. b 2. c 3. a.
Making Inferences: 1. U 2. C 3. C 4. B 5. C 6. U.
Primary Sources: 1. respectful 2. husband was Confederate general 3. sincere, warm 4. she felt the same respect.

CHAPTER 29
Word Bank: 1. a 2. b.
Parent/Partner: 1. west south west, southwest 2. Petersburg and Richmond 3. possible answers- retreating west away from Grant's army, moving away from union-controlled railroads
Primary Sources: 1. Lee 2. bravery 3. slavery 4. opinion. (discuss)

CHAPTER 30
Word Bank: 1. b 2. b.
Drawing Conclusions: 1. b 2. b 3. b.
Primary Sources: 1. Lincoln was very tall 2. acted bravely 3. mentions himself, Robert, and Senator 4. no (discuss)

CHAPTER 31
Fact or Opinion: 1. O 2. F 3. F 4. O 5. O 6. O 7. O 8. F.
Primary Source: 1. someone who does not want revenge 2. worst 3.war has ruined the region 4. opinion (discuss)

CPSIA information can be obtained at www.ICGtesting.com
Printed in the USA
BVOW06s1654101214

378562BV00001B/5/P